W9-CFH-593

fat quarter

fun

Karen Snyder

©2007 Karen Snyder

Published by

700 East State Street • Iola, WI 54990-0001
715-445-2214 • 888-457-2873
www.krausebooks.com

Our toll-free number to place an order or obtain a free catalog is (800) 258-0929.

All rights reserved. No portion of this publication may be reproduced or transmitted in any form or by any means, electronic or mechanical, including photocopy, recording, or any information storage and retrieval system, without permission in writing from the publisher, except by a reviewer who may quote brief passages in a critical article or review to be printed in a magazine or newspaper, or electronically transmitted on radio, television, or the Internet.

The following registered trademark terms and companies appear in this publication:
Andover Fabrics, Anna Lena's, Annie's Attic, Keepsake Quilting.

Library of Congress Control Number: 2007923001
ISBN-13: 978-0-89689-537-9
ISBN-10: 0-89689-537-8

Edited by Andy Belmas
Designed by Donna Mummery and Heidi Bittner-Zastrow

Printed in China

dedication

This book is dedicated to all the quilters in my life, whether they've walked through the doors of my shop, visited me online or quilt with me on a regular basis. You all inspire me!

acknowledgments

I would like to thank the many wonderful people who helped make this book possible.

Darlene Zimmerman for recommending Krause Publications and answering my many questions.

Candy Wiza for believing in me.

Andy Belmas for his editing skills.

Donna Mummery and Heidi Bittner-Zastrow for their design.

My sister, Sally Paxton and my mother, Bette Snyder for their advice on grammar and punctuation.

My dad, Sid Snyder, for passing on his work ethic.

The women who so willingly made quilts for the book, Jo Fitzsimmons, Winnie Tupper, Carol Osterholm, Grace Marko, Barbara Gramps, Patty Stoltz, Gail Messick, Pat Hall, Monica Solorio-Snow, Cortné Stricker, Janet King, Beverly Wakeman, Bonnie Kozowski and Connie Nason. How lucky I am to have so many good friends!

Joan Stoltz and Connie Nason for binding the majority of quilts in the book.

Last but not least, my husband, Bob Hamilton.

contents

In my sewing room, you'll find drawers full of fat quarters, charming bundles and stacks of fat quarters displayed on any flat surface. There are more fat quarters pinned to the design wall, auditioning for an upcoming project. I have a feeling that if I visited your sewing room, I might find the same thing! Fat quarters are so much fun to collect. The price for a fat quarter isn't much, they take up relatively little space, and it's so easy to justify just one more! Now it seems nearly every quilt shop has a Fat Quarter Frenzy at least once a year, offering 25 fat quarters for $25.00. No wonder our sewing rooms are bursting at the seams with fat quarters! You may not have a project in mind for those fat quarters when you bring them home from the shop, but you know you'll have the perfect fabric when inspiration strikes. That's where I hope to help, by providing some of that inspiration!

Besides collecting fat quarters, I love to design quilts with them, too. That led to my first book, *Bundles of Fun*. And while that book had 27 fat quarter quilts in it, I still had plenty of fat quarters left when it came time for this book. One of the simple pleasures of planning a quilt from fat quarters is how easy it is to gather fabrics for the quilt. Instead of piling up bolts of fabric to make your selections, you can audition numerous fat quarters. Now is the time to dig into your fat quarter collection or visit the fat quarter section of your favorite quilt shop and turn those fat quarters into finished quilts.

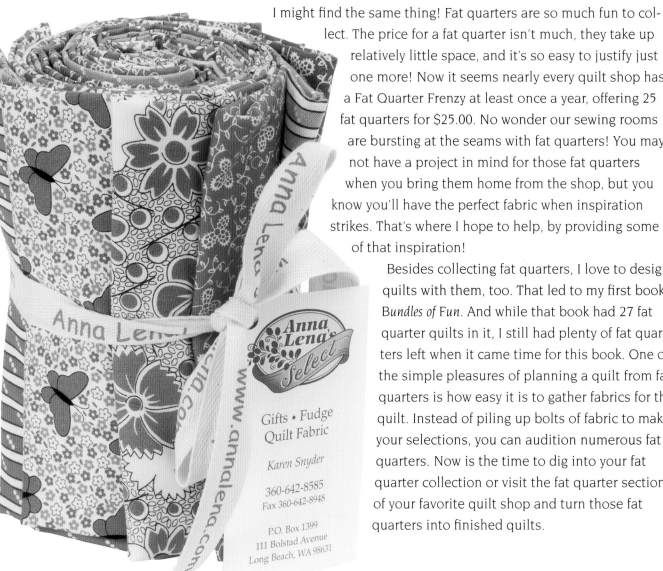

Anna Lena's Select

Gifts • Fudge
Quilt Fabric

Karen Snyder

360-642-8585
Fax 360-642-8948

P.O. Box 1399
111 Bolstad Avenue
Long Beach, WA 98631

An array of fat quarters.

what are fat quarters?

A quarter yard of fabric is 9" cut from selvage to selvage, yielding a piece approximately 9" x 42". A fat quarter is made by first cutting a half yard of fabric, or eighteen inches, from selvage to selvage. This piece is then cut in half along the fold line, yielding a piece that is approximately 18" x 22". Both pieces are equal in area, but fat quarters are often more suitable for cutting the shapes necessary for a quilt project.

why fat quarters?

Besides the fun and ease of collecting fat quarters, they have several advantages when making quilts. The pieces are easier to handle than a long, skinny ¼-yd. cut. Fat quarters are easier to stack on your cutting mat and easier to rotary cut. With fat quarters, you're making shorter cuts, and it's easier to keep your ruler stable.

When squaring up fat quarters, there is less waste. If you are squaring up a piece of fabric that is cut from selvage to selvage, you could lose 1"-2" or more of fabric. That loss is reduced when using fat quarters.

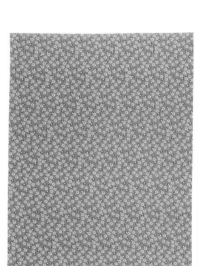

A fat quarter and a regular quarter yard of fabric have the same surface area, but fat quarters are often more suitable for cutting the patches necessary for quilting.

fabric selection

Once you've decided on a quilt pattern that you want to make, take a second look at it. Is it the fabrics that you like, or are you drawn to the design of the quilt itself? Usually the first thing we are drawn to is the palette—the colors and prints used in the quilt. If that's the case, let the photograph be your guide. However, remember that you probably aren't going to find exactly the same fabrics used in the book. Fabrics come and go quite rapidly these days, and there is so much to choose from. Fat quarter quilts are scrappy quilts, though, and substitutions shouldn't be hard to find. Having chosen a palette, you have a good jumping off point for selecting your fabrics.

If it's the quilt pattern that has attracted you, then the fabric choices are wide open. You might be guided by the personality of the recipient of the quilt or inspired by a new color combination you've seen somewhere. Look around you. Are there other quilts in combinations of colors that you like? Do you always plant red and pink flowers together? Are you attracted to magazines whose covers are graphic and bright or the ones that reflect a soft, romantic look? If there is one fabric that you're especially attracted to, let it be your inspiration and draw from it when choosing the fat quarters for your project. That special fabric often makes a good border. Keep your eyes open. Inspiration is everywhere!

No matter where you start, there are some general rules to keep in mind.

Contrast

The contrast among your fabrics can be sharp or subtle, depending on the desired result. If you choose fabrics with little contrast, the quilt will have a softer, more blended look, and the definition of the pieces and blocks will not be as clear. Most often, however, you'll want to choose fabrics with strong contrast. This will help define your work and set the design of the blocks off from their background. Contrast can be achieved by selecting fabrics with different colors or different values.

Value

The intensity of a color determines its value. You often need to find light, medium and dark fabrics to use in a quilt pattern, sometimes in the same color family. Value can be a bit tricky to determine. If you are trying to group fabric together by value, it can be helpful to lay them out from light to dark. Then, stand back and squint your eyes. An even better method is to view the fabric through a small red lens. These are available at quilt shops. The lens acts to neutralize the colors in the fabrics and lets you see just their value.

Scale

To keep your quilts interesting you should use a variety of scale in the prints. Quilters tend to gravitate toward small scale prints, since the fabric will be cut into small patches. Don't overlook medium- and large-scale prints, however, as they really add pizzazz to a quilt and keep it from being boring.

Each of the projects in this book offers suggestions on fabric selection. These are just guidelines, though, so start pulling fat quarters from your stash and let the fun begin!

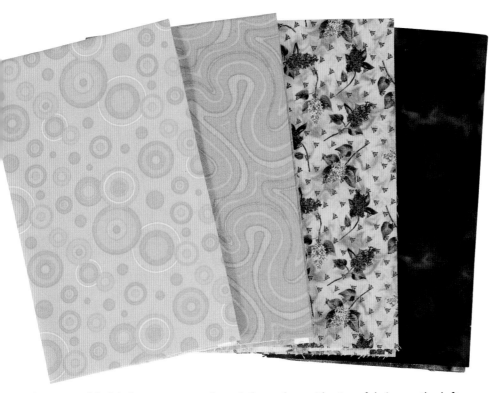

Contrast with fabric patterns can be subtle or sharp. The two fabrics on the left show subtle contrast. The two fabrics on the right show sharp contrast.

A value finder is a great aid in determining the value of a group of fabrics.

Using fabrics of various scale results in a more interesting quilt.

pre-washing fabrics

To wash or not to wash—that is the question. If you buy good, quality cotton fabric, pre-washing is not a necessity. I prefer not to wash my fabrics for a couple of reasons. First, I like the crispness of un-washed fabric. If you wash your fabrics, you remove the sizing. Secondly, I don't always have time. Often when I get a new bundle of fabrics, I just can't wait to cut into them! If I take the time to pre-wash, the inspiration may be gone. Lastly, I like the look you get when you wash a finished quilt and it puckers up just a bit around your quilting stitches.

For those of you who do pre-wash, here are some tips. Because you'll be working with fat quarters, which are relatively small pieces of fabric, you don't want to just toss them into the washer and dryer. You risk losing too much fabric due to frayed edges. Shrinkage is minimal with good quality cotton fabrics. The main reason for pre-washing is to remove any excess dye. You can do this easily without sending your fabrics for a spin in the washer and a tumble in the dryer. Follow these guidelines for pre-washing your fat quarters:

1. Fill your sink or a basin with tepid water. Put your fat quarters into the water one or two at a time, and swish them around. If you notice a lot of dye being released, change the water and repeat until the water stays clear.

2. Place your fat quarters, a few at a time, on a towel. Roll the towel around them and squeeze gently, then drape them on anything handy until they are nearly dry.

3. When the fabrics are still damp, press them with a dry iron until they are completely dry. If you waited too long, and the fabrics are completely dry, just spray them with a mist of water, wait a few minutes, then press.

4. You may want to use some spray sizing on your fabrics once you have pressed them dry. The sizing will give your fabrics body and make them easier to cut and stitch.

I've taught many beginners to quilt, and I always tell them that there are only four steps to becoming a successful quilter. Of course, you still need to quilt and bind your project, but if you pay attention to these four principles, your seams will match and your quilt top will lay flat.

- Accurate cutting

- A ¼" seam allowance

- Good pressing techniques

- Measuring through the middle when adding your borders

cutting

Accurate cutting is the first step in making quilts that go together easily and lay flat. Proper tools make cutting easy. Be sure that your rotary cutter has a sharp blade with no nicks, that you have a ruler that is at least 24" long and that your mat is free of grooves.

The most common problem when cutting is letting the ruler wiggle as you make your cut. To avoid this, spread your fingers apart and place the fingertips on the half of the ruler that is closest to you. Do not lay your palm flat on the ruler. Place your rotary cutter next to the ruler and cut about half way across your fabric. Leaving your cutter in place, walk the fingers of the hand that is on the ruler up to the half of the ruler that is farthest from you. Press downward with your fingertips and continue making the cut.

Get familiar with your cutting tools and learn to read your ruler correctly. If you are cutting a lot of strips that are the same size, it can be helpful to put a narrow piece of masking tape on the back of the ruler at the proper measurement. That way you can quickly see that you are lining up properly.

Did you know that your index finger should be

Proper placement of your fingers on the ruler and rotary cutter help insure a perfect cut.

placed on the top of your rotary cutter? Every brand of rotary cutter has a place for your index finger. If you grip your cutter like a two-year-old learning to eat with a spoon, and make your cuts with all your fingers wrapped around the handle, your wrist is twisted and your hand is in an awkward position. By placing your index finger on the top of your cutter, you have a straight line from your elbow. This is ergonomically correct and won't lead to problems with your wrist or elbow.

When working with fat quarters, you are working with fairly small pieces of fabric. Fat quarters are approximately 18" x 22". The 22" measurement, however, usually includes the selvage. This is the edge where the fabric yarns are woven back, and it needs to be trimmed off. All of the instructions in the book tell you which side of your fat quarter should be across the bottom edge of your cutting mat when you begin cutting. While you will want to even the edges of your fat quarters and trim away the selvage, be conservative when trimming.

You can speed your cutting by layering your fat quarters and cutting several at a time. For the sake of accuracy, I don't like to layer more than four fat quarters. When layering several fat quarters, align the edges with the selvage. Depending on the pattern instructions, place this edge either at the top or the right side of your cutting mat. Trim the left edge of your fat quarters so they are even before beginning your cutting.

A guide can insure an accurate ¼" seam allowance.

seam allowance

Once you've cut your pieces accurately, it is important to sew them together using a ¼" seam. Many sewing machines come with a ¼" foot, or a special ¼" foot can be purchased for them. If you do a lot of quilting, you may want to consider this. If you do not have a ¼" foot, lay your acrylic ruler under your needle. Slowly, by hand, lower your needle until it just rests on the ¼" mark. Use a piece of masking tape on your machine to mark along the edge of the ruler. Use this tape as a guide when sewing your seams.

To make sure that you are using your ¼" foot correctly, or that you have your masking tape in the correct position, do this experiment. Cut two 2" strips of fabric, about 3" long. Lay the strips together and sew along the long side with a ¼" seam. Press open. Now use your ruler to measure the width of the piece. It should be 3½". If not, make adjustments and repeat the experiment.

pressing

You want to press your fabrics and your seams without distorting them, which requires a gentle touch. Whether or not to use steam is a matter of personal preference, but be aware that you are more likely to distort your fabrics if you are using steam.

When quilting, seams are generally pressed to one side as opposed to being pressed open. When pressing seams to one side, it is very important to press from the front. Lay the pieced patches on the ironing board. Since you will usually want to press your seam toward the darker fabric, lay the pieced patch with the darker fabric on the top. This will automatically make the seam allowance lay toward the darker fabric when you separate the patches. Before opening, give the seam a quick press to help marry the sewing threads to the fabric. Then gently lift the top layer of fabric. Use the side of the iron to lay it over and press. By pressing from the front in this manner, you will avoid leaving little folds or pleats at the seams. These little pleats can have an adverse effect when you join your blocks or rows together.

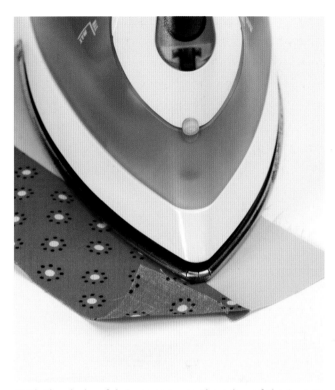

With the darker fabric on top, use the edge of the iron to gently press the top patch over.

nesting seams

When joining pieced blocks or rows together, it is a good idea to nest the seams. This is accomplished when the seam allowances in the blocks being joined are pressed in opposite directions.

If you aren't familiar with nesting seams, try this little exercise to make a four-patch block. It clearly demonstrates how nesting is done, and makes your match point perfect!

1. From scraps, cut a light and dark strip 2½" wide and at least 6" long.
2. Stitch the two strips, right sides together, along the long sides.
3. Press toward the darker fabric.
4. Cut the strip into two 2½" segments.

5. Place the two segments right sides together, matching light to dark. The seams will fall in opposite directions. You can wiggle the pieces and feel the seam allowances butt up to each other.
6. Place a pin on either side of the seam and stitch.

borders

Borders on a quilt act like a frame on a picture: they serve to contain the action going on in the body of the work. Often this can be accomplished with a narrow border of an accent fabric and a wider border that matches the tone and value of the blocks. You can also use borders to increase the size of a finished quilt. Each of the projects in the book gives you suggestions for choosing appropriate borders.

While borders may be the finishing touch to your masterpiece, if applied incorrectly, they can cause problems. If you merely cut a long strip and start sewing it to the edges of your quilt top, the border strip has a tendency to "grow," and the quilt won't lay flat. This occurs because the edges of your quilt include numerous seams which can become "unlocked" when you handle the quilt top. As you add the border to the edge of the top, each seam may open a little, causing the problem.

You can, however, create a quilt top that lays flat every time. It's as simple as measuring correctly and cutting the border strips the proper length before adding them.

After piecing and assembling the quilt blocks, find a flat surface on which to lay the finished top. Using a tape measure, measure the length of the quilt through the middle. Cut two strips of border fabric this length. Find the center of the strip and the center of the quilt top. This can be done by folding the fabric in half and finger pressing. Pin the border strip to the quilt top at the center point. Next, pin the top and bottom edge. Continue pinning every few inches, easing if necessary. Sew the seam with a ¼" seam allowance. Press toward the border fabric.

Next, you will want to measure the width of the quilt top. Again, measure through the middle to assure that your finished top will lay flat. Cut two strips of border fabric this length. Find the centers, pin, stitch and press. If there are multiple borders, repeat the steps, doing the lengthwise borders first.

Always measure through the middle of the quilt top to determine the length of the border strips.

batting

There are many choices of batting to use in your quilt. Batting can be made from natural fibers like cotton, wool, or even silk. They can also be made from polyester or a combination of a natural fiber and polyester. There are different weights, thickness and lofts to consider as well. I mostly use cotton blends as I like the flat look and ease of care that they provide. Occasionally I use a polyester batt, but I look for one that drapes well and doesn't have too much loft.

layering and basting

Once your quilt top is complete, you will need to make a quilt "sandwich" before you begin quilting. The quilt sandwich is made up of the quilt back, batting and the pieced top. The backing and batting should be at least 4" larger than the quilt top.

1. After doing any necessary piecing of the backing fabric, tape the fabric, wrong side up, to a flat surface. Take care to insure that the fabric is pulled taut.
2. Lay the batting over the backing and smooth out any wrinkles.
3. Lay the well-pressed quilt top, right side up, on top of the batting.
4. If you will be hand quilting, baste with long running stitches. If you will be machine quilting, baste with safety pins.

quilting

Quilting is the finishing touch in quilt making. All of the quilts in the book give you suggestions for quilting designs, but feel free to experiment on your own.

If you aren't experienced at quilting by hand or machine, there are many good books available on the subject.

binding

1. Cut binding strips 2¼" wide x width of fabric.
2. After cutting the required number of strips, piece them together with diagonal seams.
3. Press seams open.
4. Press the binding in half lengthwise, wrong sides together.
5. Trim excess batting and backing from quilted top.
6. Beginning in the middle of the quilt, place the folded binding strip right sides together along the edge of the quilt. The raw edges of the binding and the raw edges of the quilt should be together. Pin one side.
7. Beginning six or seven inches from the end of the binding strip, stitch with a ¼" seam. Stop stitching ¼" from the corner.
8. Backstitch.
9. Pivot the quilt. Fold the binding strip up at a 45-degree angle then back down.
10. Begin sewing at the top edge of the quilt.
11. Continue around all four corners. Stop stitching approximately 3" from the beginning of the strip. This will leave about 9" of binding unsewn.
12. In the middle of this space, fold back the loose ends of the strips so they meet.
13. Mark a dot along the fold at this point.
14. Open the binding strips.
15. Pivot, aligning the dots, and sew the strips together with a diagonal seam.
16. Trim excess binding and attach the unsewn area to quilt.
17. Fold the binding over the raw edge of the quilt so that it covers the machine stitching on the back side.
18. Stitch in place using a blind stitch. A miter will form at the corners of your quilt.

labeling

I can't stress enough how important it is to label your quilts. Have you ever had the frustration of looking through old family photograph albums and wondering about the ancestors who stare out at you from faded photographs? I feel the same way when I look at antique and vintage quilts.

Quilts have a story to tell. Even unlabeled quilts tell a story. The fabrics used in them are a clue to their age. The precision of the stitching is an indication of the maker's skill. The amount of wear tells whether the quilt was used as a utility quilt or made for display. Missing is the who, what and where. Who made the quilt? What was the occasion and where did the quiltmaker live? A simple label stitched to the back of a quilt can answer all of these questions.

Quilt labels can be simple or elaborate. A piece of muslin with the pertinent information written in permanent ink and whip stitched to the back of the quilt will suffice. If you are feeling more creative, you can embroider a label by hand or machine and embellish it with additional needlework. Photos transferred to fabric add a personal touch to a quilt. Decorative fabric labels are also available. These often have a design around the border and a blank area for you to add your personal information. Here's my favorite way to make a label.

1. Type the information you want into a word processing program on your computer. Use a font and type size that are easy to read. Type size of 16–24 is a good choice.
2. Print the information and tape the paper to a desk or table.
3. Tape an unwashed piece of muslin over the paper.
4. Using a fine-point permanent pen, trace over the letters.
5. Remove the tape. Press edges under ¼ ".
6. Stitch the label to the back of the quilt.

Future generations will thank you!

Labels can be as plain or fancy as you wish.

fun shui

While the principles of the ancient art of feng shui may not really apply to quilting, I love the fun way the background fabrics in this quilt live in harmony. The nine-patch pinwheels add order to the chaos. This quilt will bring to mind sunny days and summer breezes and add some *Fun Shui* to your life!

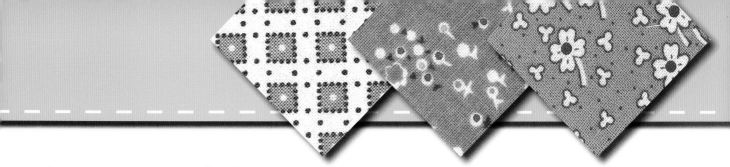

choosing fabric

In this quilt, the fat quarters become the background, and the accent fabric makes the pinwheels. By choosing fat quarters that have some pattern but not much contrast, a blended feeling is achieved. You'll want the pinwheels to stand out from the other fabrics, so choose something with good color saturation.

Don't overlook the option of using dark fabrics for the background and something light for the pinwheels. A quilt made with darker fat quarters would be nice with white pinwheels.

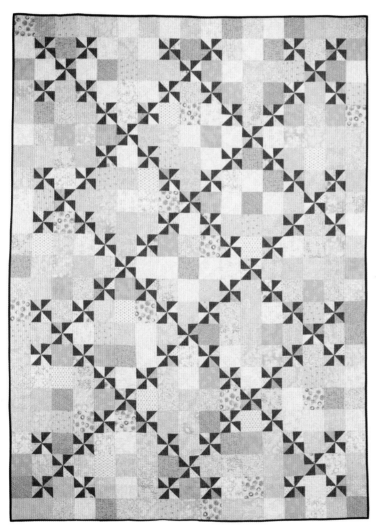

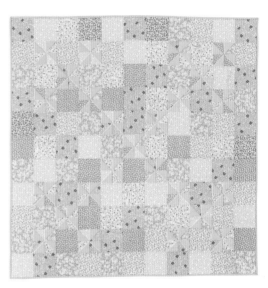

The colors chosen for this quilt are truly reminiscent of a summer's day.
Pieced and quilted by the author, 2006.

The muted tones of the fat quarters used here allow the pinwheels to "pop."
Pieced by Connie Nason and quilted by the author, 2006.

measurements

Quilt: 68" x 92"
Block size: 12"

fabric requirements

30 fat quarters
1⅓ yd. accent fabric
5⅓ yd. backing
⅔ yd. binding fabric

cutting instructions

Note: Place the 18" side of the fat quarter along the bottom edge of your cutting mat, selvage at the top.

1. From each fat quarter, cut:
   (3) 4½" strips; crosscut into (11) 4½" squares and (1) 2⅞" square
   (1) 2⅞" strip; crosscut into (6) 2⅞" squares
2. From the accent fabric, cut:
   (14) 2⅞" strips; crosscut each strip into (13) 2⅞" squares
3. From the binding fabric, cut:
   (9) 2¼" strips.

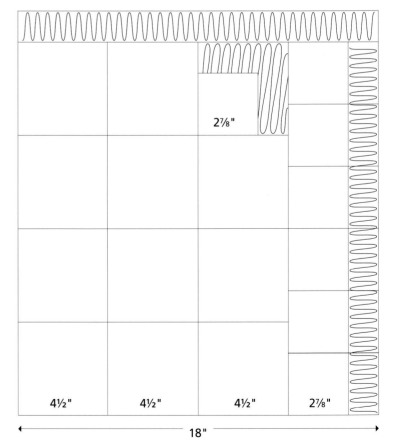

Fat quarter cutting diagram.

piecing the blocks

Pinwheel Blocks

1 Draw a diagonal line on the back of the 2⅞" accent squares.

2 Pair an accent square with a background square, right sides together, and sew ¼" on either side of the marked line.

3 Cut apart on the marked line. Press toward the darker fabric.

4 Repeat to make 180 half-square triangles.

5 Join four half-square triangles together to make a pinwheel block. Use a variety of fabric combinations. Press toward the 4½" blocks. Take care to turn all of your pinwheels in the same direction. Make 90 pinwheel blocks.

6 Join five pinwheel blocks with four 4½" squares to make a pinwheel nine-patch.

Making the half-square triangles.

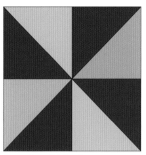

Pinwheel blocks.

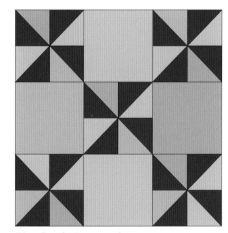

Pinwheel nine-patch.

Nine-patch Blocks

1 Join three 4½" blocks together into a row.

2 Repeat to make two more rows.

3 Press the seams in two rows toward the outside, and in one row toward the middle.

4 Join the three rows together to make a nine-patch, nesting seams.

5 Repeat to make 18 nine-patch blocks.

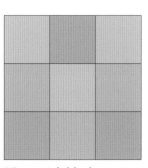

Nine-patch blocks

assembling the top

1 Lay out the blocks in seven rows of five blocks each, alternating pinwheel blocks and nine-patch blocks.

2 Join the blocks together into rows.

3 Press the seams in each row toward the nine-patch blocks. This will allow the seams in each row to nest with the seams in the row below it.

4 Join the rows together. Press.

Assembly diagram.

piecing the border

1 Join (21) 4½" blocks together for one side border. Repeat for the second side border.

2 Sew to the sides of the quilt.

3 Join (17) 4½" squares together for the top border. Repeat for the bottom border.

4 Sew to the top and bottom of the quilt.

5 Stay stitch the edge of the quilt top.

preparing the backing

1 Cut the backing fabric into two equal pieces.

2 Remove the selvage and stitch the two pieces together along the longest sides.

finishing your quilt

1 Prepare your quilt sandwich following the Layering and Basting instructions on page 15.

2 A small all-over pattern, like stippling, is very effective when used in the background of this quilt. By leaving the pinwheels unquilted, they will stand out from the rest of the quilt.

3 Bind and label your quilt following the instructions on page 16–17.

tip

Stay stitching stabilizes the edges of your quilt top. A pieced quilt top that doesn't have borders often has many seams along the edges. As you handle your quilt top while basting and quilting it, the stitching at the end of these seams has a tendency to pull apart. To stay stitch, stitch around the outside of your quilt a scant ¼" from the edge. This line of stitching will be covered when you apply your binding.

This quilt is comprised of negative and positive blocks. When set side-by-side and on point, an interesting pattern appears. Although the pieces aren't large, it was a perfect choice to show off some novelty sport prints. Baseball is always a part of our family's *Summer Fun*!

choosing fabric

As in any quilt, the contrast in the fabrics will determine whether the blocks stand out prominently from the background or blend together. In the two samples here, you can see both variations. In the small quilt, the background is also scrappy. The key to making the fabrics in the blended quilt all work together is the fact that they all have the same value, or intensity of color.

At the other end of the spectrum, this quilt could be made as a study in lights and darks. In every other block the fabrics are placed in a positive/negative arrangement. Black prints on white would be quite graphic.

Arranging the blocks by color forms a strong geometric design.
Pieced by Cortné Stricker and quilted by the author, 2006.

A more blended effect is achieved with the 'mod' fabrics in this version of Summer Fun.

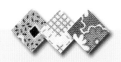

tip

When cutting multiple strips the same size, mark your ruler with a piece of masking tape or a specially designed plastic strip that clings to the back of the ruler. This will make it fast and easy to line your ruler up on your fabric, and keep you from cutting a strip the wrong size.

measurements

Quilt: 63" x 80"
Block size: 6"

fabric
requirements

9 fat quarters
2¼ yd. background fabric
⅓ yd. inner border
1⅓ yd. outer border
⅔ yd. binding
4 yd. backing

cutting instructions

Note: Place the 18" side of the fat quarter along the bottom edge of your cutting mat, selvage at the top.

1. From each fat quarter, cut:
   - (7) 2½" strips; crosscut two strips into
     - (16) 2½" squares
   - Crosscut four strips into
   - (12) 6½" x 2½" rectangles
   - Crosscut the remaining strip into
   - (3) 2½" squares
   - Note: Keep like fabrics together.
2. From the background fabric, cut:
   - (20) 2½" strips; crosscut eight strips into (118) 2½" squares
   - Crosscut twelve strips into
   - (70) 2½" x 6½" rectangles
   - (2) 9¾" strips; crosscut into (6) 9¾" squares.
   - Cut each square diagonally twice for 24 side setting triangles
   - (1) 5¼" strip; crosscut into (2) 5¼" squares
   - Cut each square once diagonally for corner triangles
3. From the inner-border fabric, cut:
   - (7) 1½" strips
4. From the outer-border fabric, cut:
   - (8) 5½" strips
5. From the binding fabric, cut:
   - (8) 2¼" strips

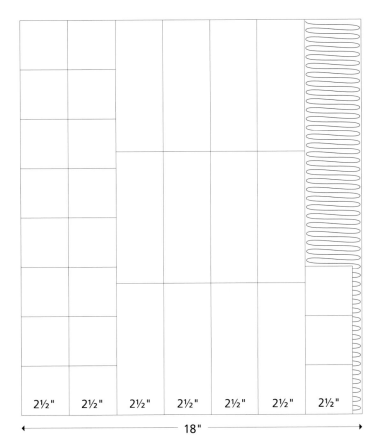

2½"   2½"   2½"   2½"   2½"   2½"   2½"

←——————————— 18" ———————————→

Fat quarter cutting diagram.

piecing the blocks

Dark blocks.

Dark Blocks

1 Using fabrics from one fat quarter, sew a 2½" print square to either side of a 2½" background square. Press toward the print.

2 Sew a 6½" x 2½" print rectangle to either side of pieced segment from Step 1. Press toward the print. Make 48.

Light blocks.

Light Blocks

3 Sew a 2½" background square to either side of a 2½" print square. Press toward the print.

4 Sew a 6½" x 2½" background rectangle to either side of pieced segment from Step 1. Press toward the print. Make 35.

assembling the top

1 Working on a design wall or on the floor, lay out the light and dark blocks, the side setting triangles and the corner triangles as shown in the assembly diagram. You may choose to arrange the blocks randomly or in a diagonal pattern.

2 Once you have the blocks laid out in a pleasing manner, join the blocks together into rows.

3 Press the seams in each row toward the print blocks. This will allow the seams in each row to nest with the seams in the row below it.

4 Join the rows together. Press.

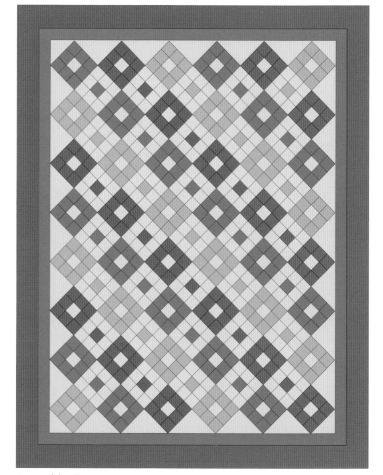

Assembly diagram.

adding the borders

1 Join the strips for the inner border together by sewing diagonal seams. Press open. Join all of the strips together until you have one long strip.

2 Measure the length of your quilt lengthwise through the middle. This will prevent you from having wavy borders. Mathematically, this number would be 68½", but everyone's seam allowances vary, so be sure to measure.

3 Cut two strips the length of your quilt.

4 Attach a strip to each side of the quilt. Press.

5 Now measure your quilt crosswise through the middle. This measurement should be approximately 53½", but check your measurement to be sure.

6 Cut two strips this length.

7 Add the strips to the top and bottom of your quilt. Press.

8 Repeat steps 1–7 with your outer-border fabric.

preparing the backing

1 Cut the backing fabric into two equal pieces.

2 Remove the selvage and stitch the two pieces together along the longest sides.

finishing your quilt

1 Prepare your quilt sandwich following the Layering and Basting instructions on page 15.

2 If you choose variegated thread when quilting, it can easily take over the quilt. However, in this instance, the reds, blues and greens of the quilting thread become a part of the pattern. Rather than stippling, an easy and effective quilting design for this pattern would be to stitch in the ditch between the blocks. The stitching lines could be continued through the borders for a nice, clean look.

3 Bind and label your quilt following the instructions on page 16–17.

This quilt is perfect for using a collection of fat quarters that are all the same color. All you need to add is a little accent fabric, and, voila! You have a quilt that is interesting and fun. It's easy to make this quilt bigger, too. Just add more fat quarters and *Let the Fun Begin*!

choosing fabric

It's important to find fat quarters for this quilt that have the same value. The quilt featured here uses a monochromatic color scheme. You might want to do the same to insure success, but as long as you pay attention to the value, you could mix up your colors. Once you've decided on your fat quarters, audition fabrics with strong contrast for the accent fabric.

The purple batiks in my collection were just crying out for a project. Pairing them with gold really added a punch!
Pieced by Jo Fitzsimmons and quilted by the author, 2006.

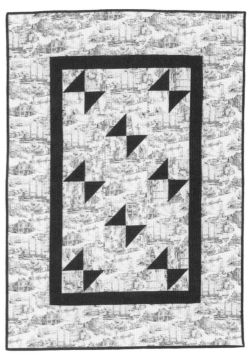

Instead of fat quarters, I used a piece of toile to make this small version of the quilt.
Pieced and quilted by the author, 2006.

tip

Value is the intensity of color, not the color itself. You can purchase a value finder to help you determine the value of your fabrics. When you look at fabrics through this little red lens, it takes away the color and lets you see if some of the fabrics are lighter or darker than others.

measurements

Quilt: 58" x 70"
Block size: 6"

fabric requirements

12 fat quarters
⅓ yd. accent fabric
½ yd. inner-border fabric
1⅓ yd. outer-border fabric
3½ yd. backing
½ yd. binding fabric

cutting instructions

Note: Place the 18" side of the fat quarter along the bottom edge of your cutting mat, selvage at the top.

1. From each fat quarter, cut:
   (1) 3⅞" strip; crosscut into (4) 3⅞" squares and (1) 3½" square
   Now, turn the fat quarter a quarter turn and cut:
   (2) 6½" strips; crosscut into (4) 6½" squares
   (1) 3½" strip; crosscut into (3) 3½" squares

Note: From each fat quarter you should have (4) 6½" squares, (4) 3⅞" squares and (4) 3½" squares. You will not need all of the 3⅞" squares and 3½" squares, so if a couple of your fat quarters are a bit short, you'll still be fine.

Because they are so similar in size, you may want to mark your 3½" and 3⅞" squares so you don't mix them up.

2. From the accent fabric, cut:
   (2) 3⅞" strips; crosscut each strip into (10) 3⅞" squares
3. From the inner border fabric, cut:
   (5) 2½" strips
4. From the outer border fabric, cut:
   (6) 6½" strips
5. From the binding fabric, cut:
   (6) 2¼" strips

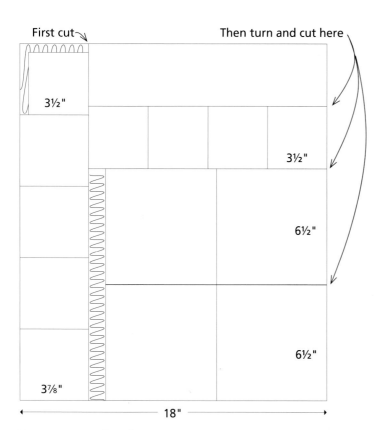

First cut

Then turn and cut here

3½"

3½"

6½"

6½"

3⅞"

18"

Fat quarter cutting diagram.

piecing the blocks

1 Draw a diagonal line on the back of the 3⅞" accent squares.

2 Pair an accent square with a print square, right sides together, and sew ¼" on either side of the marked line.

3 Cut apart on the marked line. Press toward the darker fabric.

4 Repeat to make 36 half-square triangles.

5 Join two half-square triangles together with two 3½" squares to make a four-patch block. Use a variety of fabric combinations. Press toward the 3½" squares. Make 18 four-patch blocks.

Making the half-square triangles.

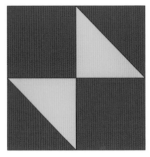

Four-patch blocks.

assembling the top

1 Work on the floor or a design wall. Using the four-patch blocks and the 6½" squares, lay out the blocks in nine rows of seven blocks each, according to the assembly diagram. Take care that all the four-patch blocks are turned in the same direction.

2 Join the blocks together into rows.

3 Press the seams in each row toward the 6½" squares. This will allow the seams in each row to nest with the seams in the row below it.

4 Join the rows together. Press.

Assembly diagram.

adding the borders

1 Join the strips for the inner border together by sewing diagonal seams. Press open. Join all of the strips together until you have one long strip.

2 Measure the length of your quilt lengthwise through the middle. This will prevent you from having wavy borders. Mathematically, this number would be 54½", but everyone's seam allowances vary, so be sure to measure.

3 Cut two strips the length of your quilt.

4 Attach a strip to each side of the quilt. Press.

5 Now measure your quilt crosswise through the middle. This measurement should be approximately 46½", but check your measurement to be sure.

6 Cut two strips this length.

7 Add the strips to the top and bottom of your quilt. Press.

8 Repeat steps 1–7 with your outer-border fabric.

preparing the backing

1 Cut the backing fabric into two equal pieces.

2 Remove the selvage and stitch the two pieces together along the longest sides.

finishing your quilt

1 Prepare your quilt sandwich following the Layering and Basting instructions on page 15.

2 Alternating horizontal and vertical quilting lines in the blocks of this quilt, as seen in the purple and gold version, is a clever technique that adds visual interest to the finished project. In the smaller quilt, stippling in the background creates a subtle result.

3 Bind and label your quilt following the instructions on page 16–17.

funny farm

I promise that making this quilt won't send you to the *Funny Farm*! However, look closely. Is the block white or is it black? This is a tessellating design in which the patterns interlock to reveal the design in both light and dark—always a fun element. This one is even more fun, because it's easy to make. Quick strip piecing speeds up the process.

choosing fabric

A monochromatic color theme works well for this quilt, like the blacks used in the quilt pictured. Any color combination that gives you sharp contrast will result in success with this quilt.

Red and white would also be a good choice. Many Red Cross quilts were made for fundraisers during World War I. Not only was the money raised by raffling these quilts put to good use, the strong geometric design of the cross made them appealing and insured that ticket sales would be brisk.

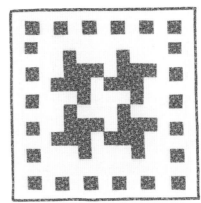

Using red and white fabric reminded me of the many Red Cross quilts that were made for fundraisers during the First World War.

Pieced by Cortné Stricker and quilted by the author, 2006.

The graphic quality of black and white is a sure winner in this quilt.
Pieced by Pat Hall and quilted by the author, 2006.

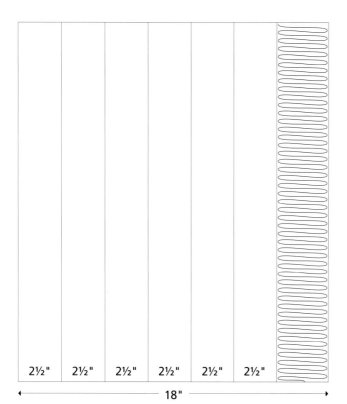

2½" 2½" 2½" 2½" 2½" 2½"

← —————— 18" —————— →

Fat quarter cutting diagram.

measurements

Quilt: 68" x 84"
Block size: 8"

fabric requirements

13 fat quarters
4 yd. background fabric
⅔ yd. binding
5 yd. backing

cutting instructions

Note: Place the 18" side of the fat quarter along the bottom edge of your cutting mat, selvage at the top.

1. From each fat quarter, cut:
   (6) 2½" strips
2. From the background fabric, cut:
   (54) 2½" strips x width of fabric
   Set aside 15 strips for borders
   Cut 39 strips in half
3. From the binding fabric, cut:
   (8) 2¼" strips x width of fabric

tip

When cutting multiple strips the same size, mark your ruler with a piece of masking tape or specially designed plastic strip that clings to the back of the ruler. This will make it fast and easy to line your ruler up on your fabric, and keep you from cutting a strip the wrong size.

piecing the blocks

1 Pair a 2½" fat quarter strip with a 2½" background strip and sew along the long side. Press toward the darker fabric. Repeat with all the fat quarter strips.

2 Set aside one strip set from each fat quarter to be used in the pieced border.

3 Cut the remaining five strip sets into 4½" segments. Keep like segments together.

Cutting the segments.

Tessellating cross block

assembling the top

1 Working on a design wall or on the floor, lay out the blocks in nine rows of seven blocks each.

2 Once you have the blocks laid out in a pleasing manner, join the blocks together into rows.

3 Press the seams in each row in opposite directions. This will allow the seams in each row to nest with the seams in the row below it.

4 Join the rows together. Press.

Assembly diagram.

borders

Note: There are three borders on this quilt—the inner border, made from the background fabric, the pieced center border and the outer border, also made from the background fabric.

Piecing the Center Border

1 Cut each of the remaining strip sets into (7) 2½" segments.

2 Join 15 segments together for the top border. Repeat for the bottom border.

3 Join 20 segments together for one side border. Repeat for the second side border.

Note: Check the length of your border strips before adding them to the quilt top. If they are too long, take a little deeper seam allowance on some squares. If too short, remove a few seams, and take a slightly smaller seam allowance.

adding the borders

1 Join the reserved background strips together for the inner border by sewing diagonal seams. Press open. Join seven strips together until you have one long strip.

2 Measure the length of your quilt lengthwise through the middle. This will prevent you from having wavy borders. Mathematically, this number would be 72½", but everyone's seam allowances vary, so be sure to measure.

3 Cut two strips the length of your quilt.

4 Attach a strip to each side of the quilt. Press toward border.

5 Now measure your quilt crosswise through the middle. This measurement should be approximately 60½", but check your measurement to be sure.

6 Cut two strips this length.

7 Add the strips to the top and bottom of your quilt. Press toward border.

8 Add the pieced center strips to the top, bottom and sides of quilt. Press toward inner border.

9 Repeat steps 1–7 with your outer-border fabric, using 8 strips.

preparing the backing

1 Cut the backing fabric into two equal pieces.

2 Remove the selvage and stitch the two pieces together along the longest sides.

finishing your quilt

1 Prepare your quilt sandwich following the Layering and Basting instructions on page 15.

2 In the black and white version of this quilt, there is only quilting in the white areas. The black areas were left unquilted, which makes them stand out. For something more fun, the red and white quilt was quilted with a spiral design. Using curved quilting designs like this can be a nice counterpoint to the strong geometry of the blocks.

3 Bind and label your quilt following the instructions on page 16–17.

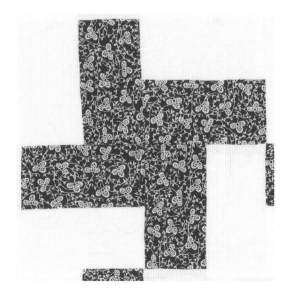

Log cabins do bring to mind **Fun and Games.** Remember the hours you spent playing with Lincoln Logs? And imagine children raised in log cabins playing old-fashioned games in front of the hearth. Or how about the fun countless quilters have had creating log cabin quilts throughout the generations!

Log cabin quilts are perennial favorites. Many young girls perfected their piecing skills stitching log cabin blocks. Antique log cabin quilts often feature red for the center block. The red is said to represent the hearth of the home. Adding the rows of strips around the hearth is like building your cabin, one log at a time! Then, once the blocks are finished, there are numerous ways to arrange them.

choosing fabric

Contrast makes the pattern of this quilt stand out. An easy way to find fabrics that contrast is to choose fabrics from two different color families, say yellow and blue. For a scrappy look a multitude of fabrics can be used and sorted by lights and darks.

The fabrics you choose will influence the feel of the finished quilt. Browns and tans will result in a quilt reminiscent of the late 1800s. You can recreate the look of a Depression Era quilt by using 1930s reproduction fabrics. For a contemporary look, batiks are a perfect choice. Or, how about pastels for a perfect baby quilt?

Borders on this quilt help stop the action created by the strong geometric design. Repeating the colors in the quilt is a good choice, or go in another direction completely and choose a large-scale print to frame the blocks.

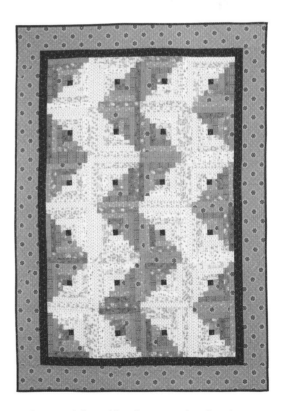

A soft, homey look results when using fabrics with warm earth tones. Here a scrap of red was used for the center of the blocks. When set like this, the blocks form a Streak of Lightning.
Pieced and quilted by the author, 2006.

Reproduction fabrics like these Wash Tub Prints create a quilt with the look of one that might have been made in the 1930s. The fabric used for the outer border is not used in the blocks, but has the same predominant colors. This is the most traditional setting for log cabin blocks and is called Barn Raising.
Pieced and quilted by the author, 2006.

measurements

Quilt: 48" x 66"
Block size: 9"

fabric requirements

12 fat quarters
⅜ yd. inner border
1 yd. outer border
3 yd. backing
½ yd. binding
52" x 70" batting

cutting instructions

Note: For both light and dark fat quarters, lay the 20" side of the fat quarter along the bottom edge of your cutting mat, selvage to the right.

From each of the dark fat quarters, cut:
  (12) 1½" strips; crosscut into:
    (4) 8½" strips
    (4) 7½" strips
    (4) 6½" strips
    (4) 5½" strips
    (4) 4½" strips
    (4) 3½" strips
    (4) 2½" strips
    (8) 1½" squares

From each of the light fat quarters, cut:
  (12) 1½" strips; crosscut into:
    (4) 9½" strips
    (4) 8½" strips
    (4) 7½" strips
    (4) 6½" strips
    (4) 5½" strips
    (4) 4½" strips
    (4) 3½" strips
    (4) 2½" strips
From the inner-border fabric, cut:
  (5) 2" strips x width of fabric
  From the outer-border fabric, cut:
  (6) 5" strips x width of fabric
  From the binding fabric, cut:
  (6) 2¼" strips x width of fabric

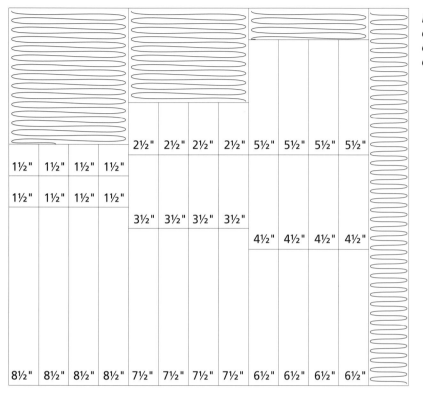

Dark fat quarter cutting diagram.

				2½"	2½"	2½"	2½"	5½"	5½"	5½"	5½"
1½"	1½"	1½"	1½"					
1½"	1½"	1½"	1½"					
				3½"	3½"	3½"	3½"	
								4½"	4½"	4½"	4½"
8½"	8½"	8½"	8½"	7½"	7½"	7½"	7½"	6½"	6½"	6½"	6½"

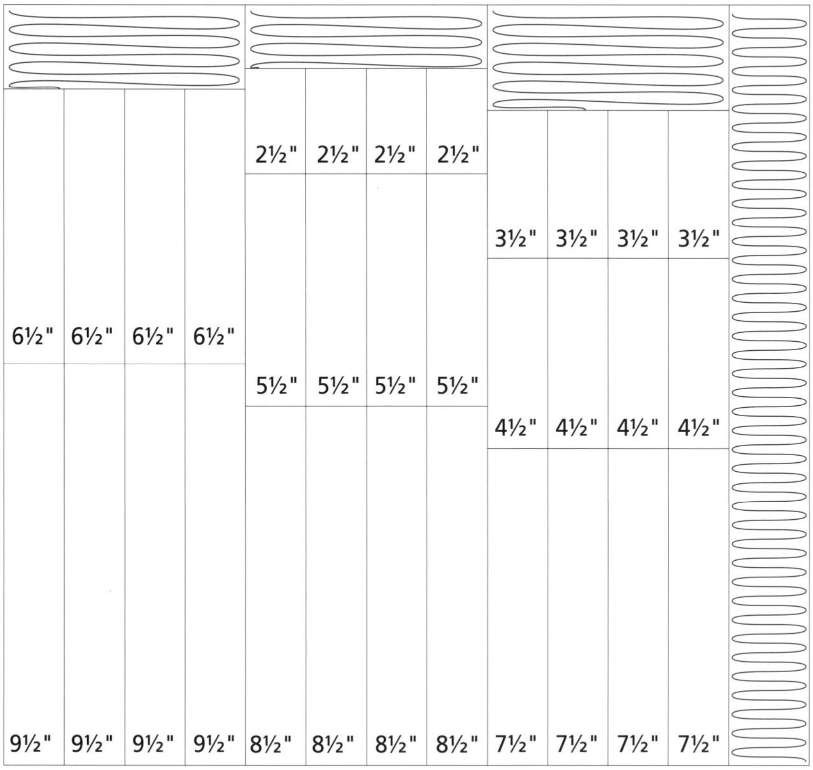

Light fat quarter cutting diagram.

				2½"	2½"	2½"	2½"	
								3½"	3½"	3½"	3½"
6½"	6½"	6½"	6½"					
				5½"	5½"	5½"	5½"	
								4½"	4½"	4½"	4½"
9½"	9½"	9½"	9½"	8½"	8½"	8½"	8½"	7½"	7½"	7½"	7½"

Center of log cabin block.

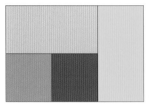

Always rotate block and add the next strip to the right.

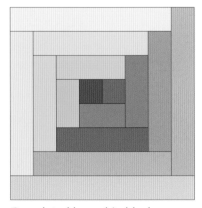

Completed log cabin block.

piecing the blocks

1 Using a variety of dark fabrics, sew 24 pairs of 1½" squares together. Press.

2 Add a 2½" dark strip to one side of the pieced segment. Press toward the 2½" strip.

3 Add a 2½" light strip to the pieced segment. Press.

Note: Strips will be added around the center in a clockwise fashion. Always press toward the most recently added strip.

4 Continue adding strips until you have gone around the center four times, using two lights, two darks, two lights, etc.

tip

When it's time to add the next strip, place the pieced segment so that the most recently added strip is at the top, add the next strip to the right, then sew. Your logs will always be in the perfect position!

assembling the top

The log cabin block can be arranged in a myriad of ways, all with colorful names that bring back memories of life on a farmstead. The directions for assembling the blocks are the same, just rearrange the blocks by rotating them. The placement of the light and dark halves of each block determine the final design. You may choose any of the designs illustrated here. You may even want to create your own.

1 Working on a design wall or on the floor, lay out the blocks in six rows of four blocks, rotating the blocks to achieve the pattern you desire (see layout diagrams).

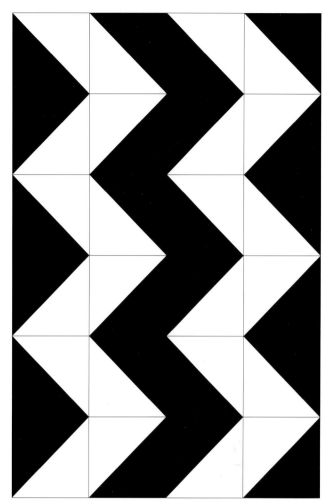

Streak of Lightning.

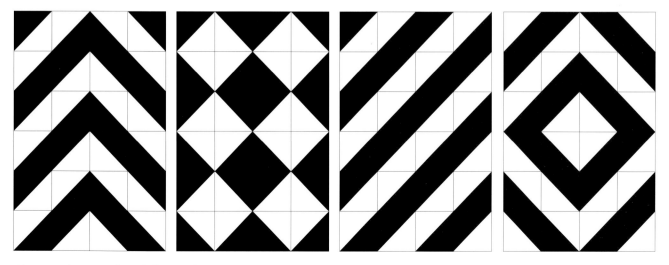

Alternate layouts, from left to right: Arrow, Dark with Light, Fields and Furrows, Barn Raising.

adding the borders

1 Join the strips for the inner border together by sewing diagonal seams. Press open. Join all of the strips together until you have one long strip.

2 Measure the length of your quilt lengthwise through the middle. This will prevent you from having wavy borders. Mathematically, this number would be 54½", but everyone's seam allowances vary, so be sure to measure.

3 Cut two strips the length of your quilt.

4 Attach a strip to each side of the quilt. Press.

5 Now measure your quilt crosswise through the middle. This measurement should be approximately 39½", but check your measurement to be sure.

6 Cut two strips this length.

7 Attach one to the top and one to the bottom of your quilt. Press.

8 Repeat steps 1–7 with your outer-border fabric.

preparing the backing

1 From the backing fabric, cut a piece 36" long. Cut this piece along the fold, yielding two sections, each approximately 22" x 36". Remove the selvages. Sew two short ends together to give you a piece approximately 22" x 71".

2 The remaining piece of backing fabric should be approximately 72" long. Split this piece along the fold, yielding two sections, each approximately 22" x 72" long. Remove the selvages. Insert the pieced section from Step 1.

finishing your quilt

1 Prepare your quilt sandwich following the Layering and Basting instructions on page 15.

2 The geometric lines of this quilt would be enhanced by cross hatching or quilting a ¼" from all seams. Alternately, a nice counterpoint to the straight lines in the quilt would be a quilting pattern with many curving lines. However you decide to quilt your quilt, be sure that the quilting design doesn't detract from the geometric pattern created by the blocks.

3 Bind and label your quilt following the instructions on page 16–17.

mutual fun

By rotating large and small triangles in just the right way, the letter "T" is formed. This is a very old block, and always a crowd pleaser. While there are several points that match up, the block is nothing more than half-square triangles.

It would be a perfect quilt for someone whose name starts with a "T" or goes to a school that starts with that letter. Even if there's no one you know that needs a 'T' quilt, don't pass this one up. The sheer graphic quality of it makes it worth adding to any collection, and the light and dark fabrics take turns forming the "T" and sharing the spotlight, having *Mutual Fun*!

choosing fabric

Part of what makes this quilt interesting is the interchanging of lights and darks in each block. To do this successfully, you'll need to be sure that there is contrast between your light fat quarters and dark fat quarters. It's okay every once in a while to throw in a fat quarter of a medium value. The design in the block created with it may not have as much definition, but an occasional rogue block can add interest to a quilt.

The quilt pictured is made with fabrics reminiscent of those found before the turn of the 20th century. This combination of warm colors and reproduction prints gives the quilt a vintage feel. For an entirely different look you could choose bright novelty prints, or go in a completely different direction and use only two colors or give the Amish palette a try, as we did in the small sample.

An Amish palette creates a very graphic quilt.
Pieced by Connie Nason and quilted by the author, 2006.

The border on this quilt is a reproduction of a 19th century "cheater" fabric. I let the colors in it be my guide for choosing the fat quarters for the quilt.
Pieced by Grace Marko and quilted by the author, 2006.

measurements

Quilt: 79" x 88"
Block size: 9"

fabric requirements

14 light fat quarters
14 dark fat quarters
⅝ yd. dark inner border
1⅔ yd. outer border
⅔ yd. binding
5¼ yd. backing

cutting instructions

Note: Place the 18" side of the fat quarter along the bottom edge of your cutting mat, selvage at the top.

1. From each fat quarter, cut:
   (1) 6⅞" strip; crosscut into (2) 6⅞" squares
   (2) 3⅞" strips; crosscut each strip into (5) 3⅞" squares
2. From the inner-border fabric, cut:
   (7) 2½" strips
3. From the outer-border fabric, cut:
   (9) 6½" strips
4. From the binding fabric, cut:
   (9) 2¼" strips

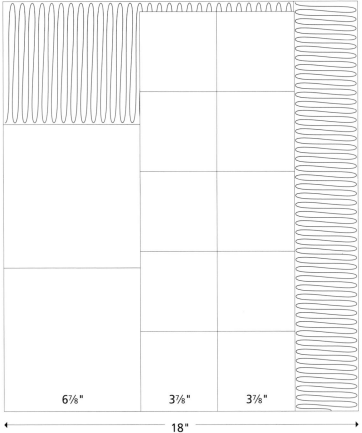

6⅞"   3⅞"   3⅞"

18"

Fat quarter cutting diagram.

piecing the blocks

1 Draw a diagonal line on the wrong side of all the light squares.

2 Work with matching light and dark fabrics for each set of blocks. Each set will yield one light and one dark block. For each set you will need 1 light and 1 dark 6⅞" square and 5 light and 5 dark 3⅞" squares.

3 Make half-square triangles by placing a light and dark square right sides together. Stitch a ¼" on each side of the drawn line.

4 Cut on the drawn line. Press toward the dark.

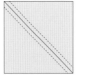

Half-square triangles.

Dark Blocks

5 Lay out one large half-square triangle block with five small half-square triangle blocks with the dark triangles pointing in. Stitch together.

Light Blocks

6 Lay out the remaining large half-square triangle block and five small half-square triangle blocks with the light triangles pointing in. Stitch together.

7 Repeat steps 2–7 to make 28 light and 28 dark blocks.

Dark block.

Light block.

assembling the top

1 Working on a design wall or on the floor, lay out the blocks in eight rows of seven blocks. Alternate light and dark blocks.

Note: In the quilt pictured, every other block changes direction. You may follow this example or experiment with your own layout.

2 Once you have the blocks laid out in a pleasing manner, join the blocks together into rows.

3 Press the seams in each row in opposite directions. This will allow the seams in each row to nest with the seams in the row below it.

4 Join the rows together. Press.

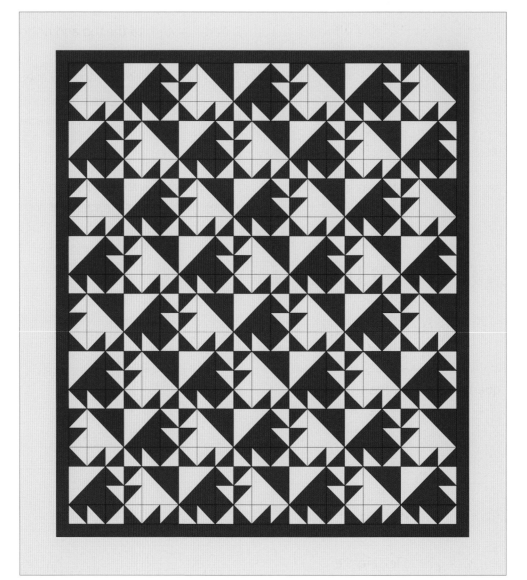

Assembly diagram.

adding the borders

1 Join the strips for the contrasting inner border together by sewing diagonal seams. Press open. Join all of the strips together until you have one long strip.

2 Measure the length of your quilt lengthwise through the middle. This will prevent you from having wavy borders. Mathematically, this number would be 72½", but everyone's seam allowances vary, so be sure to measure.

3 Cut two strips the length of your quilt.

4 Attach a strip to each side of the quilt. Press toward border.

5 Now measure your quilt crosswise through the middle. This measurement should be approximately 67½", but check your measurement to be sure.

6 Cut two strips this length.

7 Add the strips to the top and bottom of your quilt. Press toward border.

8 Repeat steps 1–7 with the outer-border fabric.

preparing the backing

1 Cut the backing fabric into two equal pieces.

2 Remove the selvage and stitch the two pieces together along the longest sides.

finishing your quilt

1 Prepare your quilt sandwich following the Layering and Basting instructions on page 15.

2 In the Amish version of this quilt, you will see stitching a quarter inch from the seams in the "Ts," and a feather design in the borders. It is also stitched in the ditch between the blocks. All of the light areas of the larger quilt were first quilted with an off-white thread. Then a dark brown thread was used to quilt in the dark areas. This way, the stippling doesn't distract from the design.

3 Bind and label your quilt following the instructions on page 16–17.

The traditional Jewel Box pattern is a stunning beauty. Here, it comes to life with fiery color. The intricate look belies the fact that it's made with nothing but half-square triangles and four-patches—easy enough for a beginner but interesting enough to please an experienced quilter! The addition of a patchwork border and scrappy binding adds interest to the finished quilt.

choosing fabric

As the traditional Jewel Box name implies, rich jewel tones are perfect for this quilt. You can stick to a narrow range of colors, as we did with the black, red and orange version, or you can let yourself go and use every bright color you can find. Just be sure to sprinkle them evenly throughout your quilt. While you may use a variety of colors, keep in mind that you'll want all of your fat quarters to have the same value. Non-directional prints are best for this pattern.

Remember, too, that your background fabric doesn't always have to be white or black. The yellow used here really makes the other fabrics pop!

You could move in a completely different direction than jewel tones. 1930s reproduction fabrics are often used successfully for this quilt. The clear pastels associated with the 1930s look cheerful on a white background.

These rich holiday fabrics lend an elegant look to the quilt.
Pieced and quilted by the author, 2006.

The hot colors in this quilt really make a statement!
Pieced by Janet King and quilted by the author, 2006.

measurements

Quilt: 80" x 100"
Block size: 20"

fabric requirements

20 fat quarters for blocks and binding
5½ yd. background and border fabric
6 yd. backing

cutting instructions

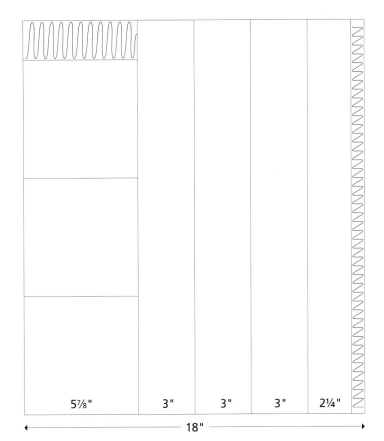

Fat quarter cutting diagram.

Note: Place the 18" side of the fat quarter along the bottom edge of your cutting mat, selvage at the top.

1. From each fat quarter, cut:
   (1) 5⅞" strip; crosscut into (3) 5⅞" squares. Set aside four squares for border.
   (3) 3" strips for 4-patch blocks
   (1) 2¼" strip for binding

2. From the background fabric, cut:
   (8) 5⅞" strips; crosscut each strip into (6)
      5⅞" squares
   (48) 3" strips
   Set 18 strips aside for the borders.
   Cut the remaining 30 strips in half.

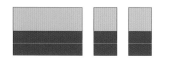

Strip piecing and cutting segments.

 Making the four-patch blocks.

Making the half-square triangles.

Quarter block.

Finished block 20" x 20".

piecing the blocks

Four-Patch Blocks

1 Pair a background strip with a fat quarter strip. Join along the long side. Press toward the darker fabric.

2 Cut into (6) 3" segments.

3 Repeat until you have used all the 3" fat quarter strips.

4 Randomly join segments into four-patch squares. Make 96.

Note: The other two-patch segments will be used in the border.

Half-Square Triangles

1 Draw a diagonal line on the wrong side of the 5⅞" background squares.

2 Pair a background square with a print square, right sides together, and sew ¼" on either side of the marked line.

3 Cut apart on the marked line. Press toward the print.

4 Repeat with all the squares, making 96 half-square triangles.

Quarter Blocks

1 Join two four-patch blocks and two half-square triangles to make a quarter block. Be sure the dark triangles are facing out and the dark squares in the four-patch blocks form a diagonal line.

2 Repeat to make 48 quarter blocks.

Blocks

1 Join four quarter blocks, being sure the dark triangles are on the outside corners and form a square in the middle.

2 Make 12.

Assembly diagram.

assembling the top

1 Lay out the blocks in four rows of three blocks each.

2 Join the blocks together into rows.

3 Press the seams in each row in opposite directions. This will allow the seams in each row to nest with the seams in the row below it.

4 Join the rows together. Press.

tip

When laying out the blocks for a scrappy quilt, don't agonize too much over the placement of the fabrics. You will want the different fabrics spread out throughout the quilt, but it's okay if two like fabrics touch occasionally. Once you have placed the blocks in a manner which seems pleasing, step away for a few minutes. When you come back, you may see something you didn't notice before.

piecing the center border

1 Using the two-patches, join 26 segments together for the top border. Repeat for the bottom border.

2 Join 34 segments together for one side border. Repeat for the second side border. Set aside.

adding the borders

1 Join (8) 3" strips together for the inner border by sewing diagonal seams. Press open.

2 Measure the length of your quilt lengthwise through the middle. This will prevent you from having wavy borders. Mathematically, this number would be 80½", but everyone's seam allowances vary, so be sure to measure.

3 Cut two strips the length of your quilt.

4 Attach a strip to each side of the quilt. Press toward the border.

5 Now measure your quilt crosswise through the middle. This measurement should be approximately 65½", but check your measurement to be sure.

6 Cut two strips this length.

7 Add the strips to the top and bottom of your quilt. Press toward the border.

8 Add a pieced strip to each side of the quilt. Press toward the inner border.

9 Trim (4) leftover 5⅞" squares to 5½". Add a 5½" square to each end of the remaining pieced borders. Join to the top and bottom of the quilt. Press toward the inner border.

10 Repeat steps 1–7 with your outer-border fabric, using 10 strips.

Note: Check the length of your border strips before adding them to the quilt top. If they are too long, take a little deeper seam allowance on some squares. If too short, remove a few seams, and take a slightly smaller seam allowance.

preparing the backing

1 Cut the backing fabric into two equal pieces.

2 Remove the selvage and stitch the two pieces together along the longest sides.

finishing your quilt

1 Prepare your quilt sandwich following the Layering and Basting instructions on page 15.

2 An allover feather pattern didn't seem to distract from the pattern of this quilt. Perhaps the vibrant colors helped support such a busy pattern.

3 Using a diagonal seam, join the 2¼" strips cut from fat quarters for binding. Bind and label following the instructions on page 16–17.

The beauty of this quilt is that it's made entirely of triangles. That's why **It's Fundamental**! And the method for making the triangles makes the construction simple and unique. By drawing a grid on paper and using it as a stitching guide, you can produce multiple half-square triangles in no time at all—and they are perfectly accurate. Make your life even easier and use purchased triangle papers.

choosing fabric

The half-square triangles in this quilt will be set to form a design borrowed from the versatile log cabin called Barn Raising. In order to assure that the design is apparent, strong contrast between the two sides of the triangle is important. If you keep all the fat quarters the same value, and choose something lighter or darker for the background, you'll be assured success.

This quilt would be stunning made with black and white fat quarters set with red. It would also be a good candidate for using the school colors when making a quilt for your favorite student.

The contrast between light and dark aren't as strong in this small version of the quilt, but still obvious enough for the design to come through.
Pieced and quilted by the author, 2006.

When the blue and white nautical prints used here were set together, they reminded me of ripples created in a lake when a stone is tossed in. The sharp contrast between dark and light really lets the design of this quilt stand out.

Pieced by Barbara Gramps and quilted by the author, 2006.

measurements

Quilt: 48" x 66"
Block size: 3"

fabric requirements

14 fat quarters
Note: you could use fat eights for this project if they are cut 10" x 18".
2¼ yd. background
⅓ yd. dark inner border
1¼ yd. outer border
½ yd. binding
3 yd. backing

cutting instructions

1. Cut each fat quarter into a 10" x 18" rectangle
Note: You will have a fat eights left over from each print. You can use these for another project, or make a second It's Fundamental quilt!
2. From the background fabric, cut (4) 18" strips; crosscut each strip into (4) 10" x 18" rectangles
3. From the inner-border fabric, cut (5) 2" strips
4. From the outer-border fabric, cut (7) 5" strips
5. From the binding fabric, cut (6) 2¼" strips

piecing the blocks

Note: Since this quilt is made entirely of half-square triangles, using a grid to piece them will save time and insure accuracy. You can draw the grid yourself, or take advantage of the triangle papers that are on the market and readily available at quilt shops. If you are using purchased triangle papers, skip the section on Drawing a Grid.

drawing a grid

Note: An 8½" x 17" piece of copy paper works perfectly for this grid. The lighter the paper, the easier it will be to remove.

1 Draw a 7¾" x 15½" rectangle.

2 Divide the rectangle into 3⅞" squares. You will have a grid that is two squares by four squares.

3 Draw diagonal lines through the squares as shown. Repeat to make 14 grids.

Note: Once you have drawn one grid, you can reproduce the rest on a copy machine. Just make sure the copy machine doesn't distort the size.

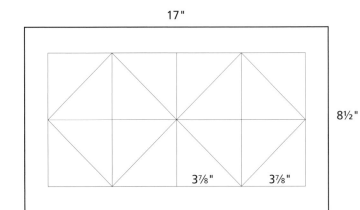

Drawing the grid.

piecing the blocks

1 Place a print fat quarter right sides together with a background fat quarter.

2 Pin the gridded paper to the fat quarters, using a pin in each triangle section.

3 Stitch ¼" on each side of the diagonal lines.

4 Cut apart on the inner lines to create your half-square triangles.

5 Press toward the darker triangles.

6 Repeat with each of the fat quarters. You will have 224 triangles.

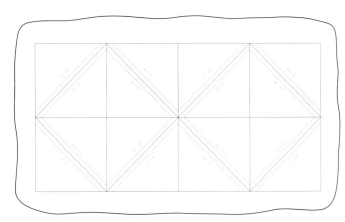

Using the triangle papers.

assembling the top

1 Working on a design wall or on the floor, lay out the blocks in eighteen rows of twelve blocks. Refer to the assembly diagram. You may find it easiest to start your layout from the middle, turning four blocks so the darker fabrics meet in the middle. Be sure to sprinkle your different fabrics evenly throughout the design.

2 Once you have the blocks laid out in a pleasing manner, join the blocks together into rows.

3 Press the seams in each row in opposite directions. This will allow the seams in each row to nest with the seams in the row below it.

4 Join the rows together. Press.

Assembly diagram.

adding the borders

1 Join the strips for the inner border together by sewing diagonal seams. Press open. Join all of the strips together until you have one long strip.

2 Measure the length of your quilt lengthwise through the middle. This will prevent you from having wavy borders. Mathematically, this number would be 54½", but everyone's seam allowances vary, so be sure to measure.

3 Cut two strips the length of your quilt.

4 Attach a strip to each side of the quilt. Press.

5 Now measure your quilt crosswise through the middle. This measurement should be approximately 39½", but check your measurement to be sure.

6 Cut two strips this length.

7 Add the strips to the top and bottom of your quilt. Press.

8 Repeat steps 1–7 with the outer-border fabric.

preparing the backing

1 Cut the backing fabric into two equal pieces.

2 Remove the selvage and stitch the two pieces together along the longest sides.

finishing your quilt

1 Prepare your quilt sandwich following the Layering and Basting instructions on page 15.

2 In a quilt with strong contrast, like the blue and white one shown here, it's a good idea to use different colored thread in the light and dark areas if you machine quilt. Hand quilting a quarter inch from the diagonal seams would be a beautiful finish for this quilt.

3 Bind and label your quilt following the instructions on page 16–17.

fun in the sun

Half-square triangles can be so versatile, as seen in this quilt. If half-square triangles aren't usually your favorite thing to make, then try this quilt, as they are pieced using triangle papers that assure accuracy! Using this method will speed your piecing tremendously, and you'll have time to enjoy some *Fun in the Sun*! This is a perfect "stash" quilt, so quit hoarding those fat quarters and let them see the light of day!

choosing fabric

Picking fat quarters for this quilt is easy, as almost anything goes. Maybe you have a basket full of novelty prints, like the fun, beach-y ones we used in the sample quilt. I find it so fun to take a peek into other people's sewing rooms to see what types of fabric they collect. Perhaps it's dog prints or frog prints or pretty florals. Maybe it's wild polka dots—not just your ordinary white dots. Take a look in your stash. What does it say about you?

Once you've chosen sixteen fat quarters, find a background fabric that will stand out from them. Maybe it's something darker or lighter, or maybe a color that you can pull from the fat quarters. Whatever you choose, give the grid method a try.

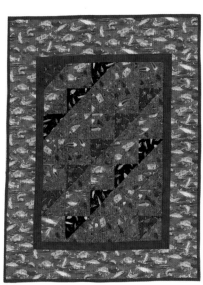

Novelty fishing prints seemed a perfect choice for a "guy" quilt.
Pieced and quilted by the author, 2006.

The bright colors in these fabrics will put you in a happy mood!
Pieced by Winnie Tupper and quilted by the author, 2006.

measurements

Quilt: 56" x 68"
Block size: 3"

fabric requirements

16 fat quarters
Note: you could use fat eights for this project if
they are cut 10" x 18".
2¼ yd. background
¼ yd. dark inner border
1½ yd. outer border
½ yd. binding
3⅓ yd. backing

cutting instructions

1. Cut each fat quarter into a 10" x 18" rectangle
Note: you will have a fat eights left over from each
print. You can use these for another project, or
make a second Fun in the Sun quilt!
2. From the background fabric, cut (4) 18" strips;
   crosscut each strip into (4) 10" x 18" rectangles
3. From the inner-border fabric, cut (5) 1½" strips
4. From the outer-border fabric, cut (8) 6½" strips
5. From the binding fabric, cut (6) 2¼" strips

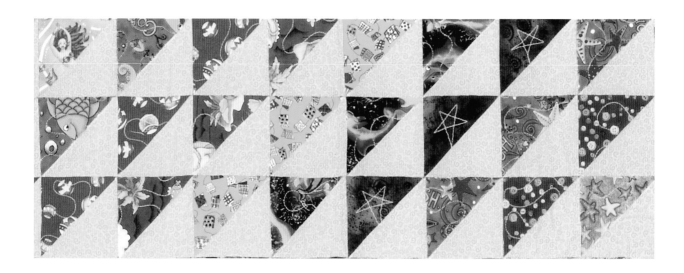

piecing the blocks

Note: Since this quilt is made entirely of half-square triangles, using a grid to piece them will save time and insure accuracy. You can draw the grid yourself, or take advantage of the triangle papers that are on the market and readily available at quilt shops. If you are using purchased triangle papers, skip the section on Drawing a Grid.

drawing a grid

Note: An 8½" x 17" piece of copy paper works perfectly for this grid. The lighter the paper, the easier it will be to remove.

1 Draw a 7¾" x 15½" rectangle.

2 Divide the rectangle into 3⅞" squares. You will have a grid that is two squares by four squares.

3 Draw diagonal lines through the squares as shown. Repeat to make 16 grids.

Note: Once you have drawn one grid, you can reproduce the rest on a copy machine. Just make sure the copy machine doesn't distort the size.

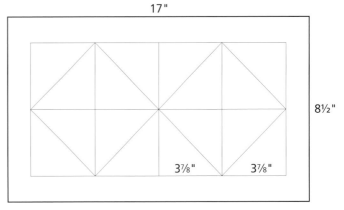

Drawing the grid.

piecing the blocks

1 Place a print fat quarter right sides together with a background fat quarter.

2 Pin the gridded paper to the fat quarters, using a pin in each triangle section.

3 Stitch ¼" on either side of the diagonal lines.

4 Cut apart on the inner lines to create your half-square triangles.

5 Press toward the darker triangles.

6 Repeat with each of the fat quarters. You will have 256 triangles.

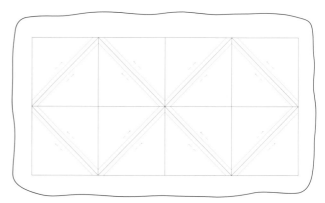

Using the triangle papers.

assembling the top

Note: The blocks will be laid out so that a diagonal pattern is formed.

1 Working on a design wall or on the floor, lay out the blocks in eighteen rows of fourteen blocks. Refer to the assembly diagram, and step back occasionally to see that the diagonal design is in alignment.

2 Once you have the blocks laid out in a pleasing manner, join them together into rows.

3 Press the seams in each row in opposite directions. This will allow the seams in each row to nest with the seams in the row below it.

4 Join the rows together. Press.

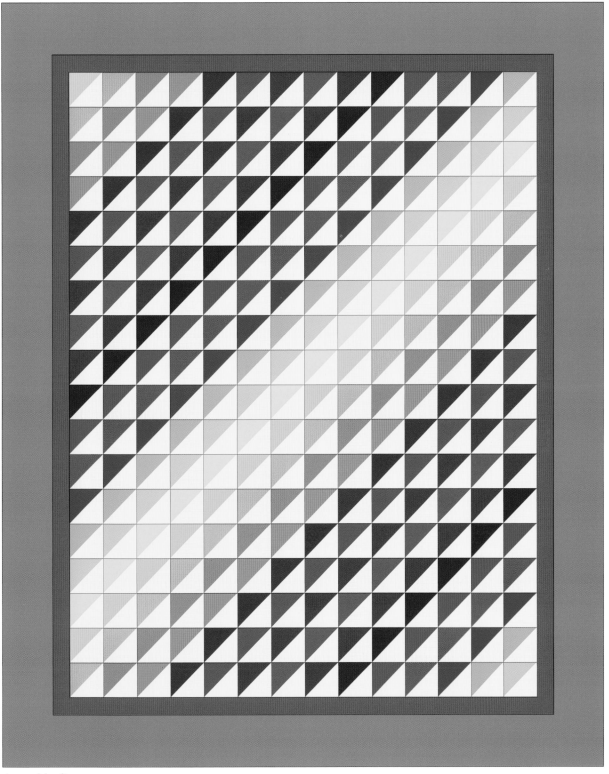

Assembly diagram.

adding the borders

1 Join the strips for the inner border together by sewing diagonal seams. Press open. Join all of the strips together until you have one long strip.

2 Measure the length of your quilt lengthwise through the middle. This will prevent you from having wavy borders. Mathematically, this number would be 54½", but everyone's seam allowances vary, so be sure to measure.

3 Cut two strips the length of your quilt.

4 Attach a strip to each side of the quilt. Press.

5 Now measure your quilt crosswise through the middle. This measurement should be approximately 44½", but check your measurement to be sure.

6 Cut two strips this length.

7 Add the strips to the top and bottom of your quilt. Press.

8 Repeat steps 1–7 with the outer-border fabric.

preparing the backing

1 Cut the backing fabric into two equal pieces.

2 Remove the selvage and stitch the two pieces together along the longest sides.

finishing your quilt

1 Prepare your quilt sandwich following the Layering and Basting instructions on page 15.

2 An allover design works well on a fun quilt like this. If you enjoy stitching in the ditch, you could follow all the diagonal lines in the quilt, continuing them into the borders.

3 Bind and label your quilt following the instructions on page 16–17.

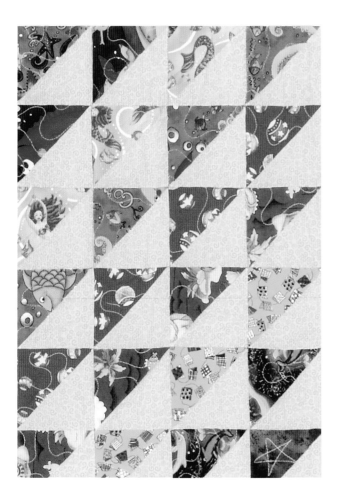

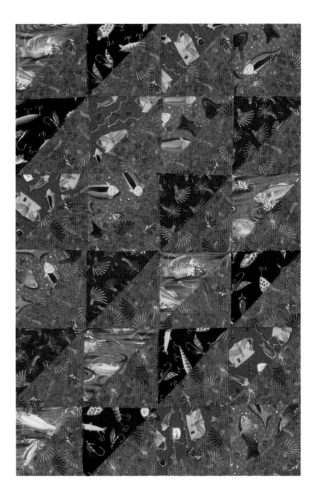

I love the sunny, crisp days of fall. When the breeze begins to blow the autumn leaves around, my thoughts always turn to the colors of the season. This pattern lets you take those colors and sprinkle them across the top of a quilt that will remind you of fall all year long. And the Fun Factor? No little stems to piece or appliqué in this quilt!

choosing fabric

The obvious choice here is a color palette of warm autumn hues, and such a choice will surely make a beautiful quilt. Within that palette, however, you have many choices. You may choose to use pale peach tones and yellow-greens. Perhaps a combination of rich browns and rusts would better suit you. Of course, there are the red, burgundy and purple colors that may call to you. Or, do like we did and combine them all!

You can also alter the look of your quilt by changing the background. Instead of a cream or tan background, why not keep your leaf colors in the lighter range of the autumn palette and use a dark background. Such a quilt would be stunning.

You may also step completely outside the range of fall colors. I once quilted a quilt for a woman who used icy blues to make her leaf blocks. The finished quilt was absolutely gorgeous.

The focus in our table runner is a dramatic purple.
The instructions for the table runner are included.
Pieced by Gail Messick and quilted by Joan Stoltz, 2006.

We chose as many fall tones as we could find for this cozy quilt.
Pieced by Bonnie Kozowski and quilted by the author, 2006.

measurements

Quilt: 70" x 87"
Block size: 9"

fabric requirements

16 fat quarters
2¾ yd. background and inner border
1⅝ yd. outer border
⅔ yd. binding
5¼ yd. backing

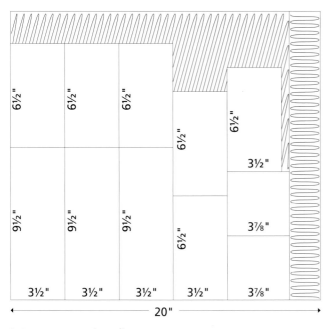

Fat quarter cutting diagram.

cutting instructions

Note: Place the 20" side of the fat quarter along the bottom edge of your cutting mat, selvage at the right.

1. From each fat quarter, cut:
   - (4) 3½" strips; crosscut the strips into
     - (3) 3½" x 9½" rectangles
     - (6) 3½" x 6½" rectangles
   - (1) 3⅞" strip; crosscut the strip into
     - (2) 3⅞" squares
2. From the background fabric, cut:
   - (18) 3½" strips; crosscut each strip into
     - (11) 3½" squares.

   You will use 192 squares.
   - (3) 3⅞" strips; crosscut each strip into
     - (10) 3⅞" squares.

   You will use 24 squares.
   - (7) 2½" strips for inner border
3. From the outer-border fabric, cut:
   - (8) 6½" strips
4. From the binding fabric, cut:
   - (8) 2¼" strips

9" strips.

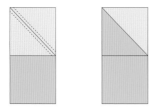

6" strips.

Reversed 6" strips.

Half-square triangles.

piecing the blocks

1 Mark a diagonal line on the back of (144) 3½" squares.

2 Place a marked square on one end of a 9½" strip with right sides together. Be sure marked line starts at the bottom left and goes to the top right. Sew on marked line. Trim, leaving a ¼" seam allowance. Press. Make 48.

3 Place a marked square on one end of a 6½" strip with right sides together. Be sure marked line starts at the bottom left and goes to the top right. Sew on marked line. Trim, leaving a ¼" seam allowance. Press. Make 48.

4 Place a marked square on one end of a 6½" strip with right sides together. This time, the marked line should start at the top left and end at the bottom right. Sew on marked line. Trim, leaving a ¼" seam allowance. Press. Make 48.

5 Mark a diagonal line on the back of (24) 3⅞" squares.

6 Place a marked 3⅞" square onto a print 3⅞" square with right sides together. Sew ¼" on either side of the marked line. Cut apart. Press. Make 48.

7 Join a 3½" background square with a half-square triangle. Check for direction of the dark side of the triangle.

8 Add a 6" strip to the left side of the unit from Step 7.

9 Add a reverse 6" strip to the bottom of the unit.

10 Add a 9" strip to the left.

11 Repeat Steps 7–10 to make 48 blocks.

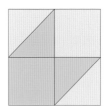
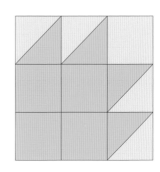

tip

Sew-and-flip corners are an easy way to add a triangle to the corner of another piece of fabric without worrying about the stretch of a bias edge.

You will need to make a mark or guide on the small squares of fabric used for the corners. You may do this by using a pencil and ruler and drawing a diagonal line on each square, or you may press each square in half diagonally and let the crease be your guide. You may also place a small piece of masking tape on the bed of your sewing machine, straight out from your needle, and let it be your guide.

The small square of fabric is then placed on the corner of the larger patch, and a diagonal line is sewn across the small patch. The corner is trimmed away, leaving a quarter-inch seam allowance. (This can be done with scissors or your rotary cutter.) The triangle that remains is pressed over to replace the fabric that was cut away.

assembling the top

1 Working on a design wall or on the floor, lay out the blocks in eight rows of six blocks each. You may choose to lay the blocks out so they all face in the same direction, alternate direction in each row, or randomly, as shown in the pictured quilt.

2 Once you have the blocks laid out in a pleasing manner, join the blocks together into rows.

3 Press the seams in every other row in the opposite direction. This will allow the seams in each row to nest with the seams in the row below it.

4 Join the rows together. Press.

Assembly diagram.

adding the borders

1 Join the strips for the inner border together by sewing diagonal seams. Press open. Join all of the strips together until you have one long strip.

2 Measure the length of your quilt lengthwise through the middle. This will prevent you from having wavy borders. Mathematically, this number would be 72½", but everyone's seam allowances vary, so be sure to measure.

3 Cut two strips the length of your quilt.

4 Attach a strip to each side of the quilt. Press.

5 Now measure your quilt crosswise through the middle. This measurement should be approximately 48½", but check your measurement to be sure.

6 Cut two strips this length.

7 Add the strips to the top and bottom of your quilt. Press.

8 Repeat steps 1–7 with your outer-border fabric.

preparing the backing

1 Cut the backing fabric into two equal pieces.

2 Remove the selvage and stitch the two pieces together along the longest sides.

finishing your quilt

1 Prepare your quilt sandwich following the Layering and Basting instructions on page 15.

2 On the large quilt, I chose to do a curving design that mimicked the wind blowing leaves about on a blustery day. It would also be very nice to quilt

¼" inside each leaf and stipple the background.

3 Bind and label your quilt following the instructions on page 16–17.

This table runner would look great gracing your table in the fall. But don't overlook using table runners in places other than the kitchen and dining room. How about along the back of a sofa or on a sofa table? You can also use a table runner on a mantel. It only takes two fat quarters and some border fabric to make this little gem.

choosing fabric

All you need for this project is two fat quarters—one for the leaves and one for the background—and a border fabric. Pick a leaf color you like for the blocks and a neutral background. For your border, go slightly lighter or darker than your leaves, or choose a different color from the fall palette.

Luckily, the range of fall colors is broad. Don't feel limited to a rusty red—your reds could lean more toward purple. Or go the other direction on the color wheel and choose something in the orange family. Keep going around the color wheel and you'll find yellow and then green. Any of these colors would be perfect for this project.

measurements

Runner 15" x 52"
Block size: 9"

fabric requirements

2 fat quarters
1⅓ yd. border and backing
⅓ yd. binding

cutting instructions

Leaf

Note: Place the 20" side of the fat quarter along the bottom edge of your cutting mat, selvage at the right.

1. From the leaf fat quarter, cut:
   - (4) 3½" strips; crosscut the strips into
     - (3) 3½" x 9½" rectangles
     - (6) 3½" x 6½" rectangles
   - (1) 3⅞" strip; crosscut the strip into (2) 3⅞" squares

Background

Note: Place the 18" side of the fat quarter along the bottom edge of your cutting mat, selvage at the top.

2. From the background fat quarter, cut:
   - (2) 3" strips; crosscut the strips into (4) 3" x 9½" rectangles
   - (2) 3½" strips; crosscut the strips into (10) 3½" squares
   - (1) 3⅞" strip; crosscut the strip into (2) 3⅞" squares and (2) 3½" squares

3. From the border/backing fabric, cut:
   - (2) 3½" strips
   - (2) 18" strips

     Set one 18" piece aside

     Crosscut the other 18" strip in half to make two pieces approximately 18" x 20". Set one aside.

     From the other piece cut a 15⅞" square.

     Cut once diagonally.

4. From the binding fabric, cut:
   - (4) 2¼" strips

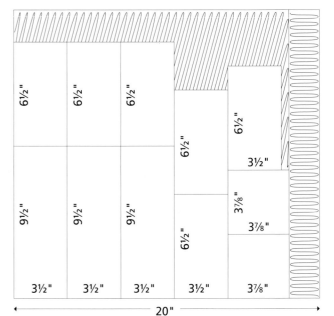

piecing the blocks

Note: You will use the sew-and-flip technique for making the segments in these blocks. For more information on sew-and-flip, see page 85.

1 Mark a diagonal line on the wrong side of the 3½" background squares.

2 Place a marked square on one end of a 9½" strip with right sides together. Be sure marked line starts at the bottom left and goes to the top right. Sew on marked line. Trim, leaving a ¼" seam allowance. Press. Make 3.

3 Place a marked square on one end of a 6½" strip with right sides together. Be sure marked line starts at the bottom left and goes to the top right. Sew on marked line. Trim, leaving a ¼" seam allowance. Press. Make 3.

4 Place a marked square on one end of a 6½" strip with right sides together. This time, the marked line should start at the top left and end at the bottom right. Sew on marked line. Trim, leaving a ¼" seam allowance. Press. Make 3.

5 Mark a diagonal line on the back of (24) 3⅞" squares.

6 Place a marked 3⅞" square onto a print 3⅞" square with right sides together. Sew ¼" on either side of the marked line. Cut apart. Press. Make 4 (you will only use 3).

9" strips.

6" strips.

Reversed 6" strips.

Half-square triangles.

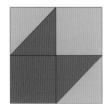

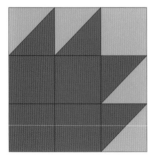

7 Join a 3½" background square with a half-square triangle. Check for direction of the dark side of the triangle.

8 Add a 6" strip to the left side of the unit from Step 7.

9 Add a Reverse 6" strip to the bottom of the unit.

10 Add a 9" strip to the left.

11 Repeat Steps 7–10 to make 3 blocks.

Leaf block.

assembling the top

1 Join the three blocks together with a 3" x 9½" strip of background fabric between them and at each end. Orient the blocks as shown in the illustration or to your liking. Press toward the background strips.

2 Measure the length of your runner lengthwise through the middle. This will assure that your runner lays flat. Mathematically, this number would be 39½", but everyone's seam allowances vary, so be sure to measure.

3 Cut two strips the length of your runner.

4 Attach a strip to each side. Press.

5 Add a large triangle to each end of the runner, taking care not to stretch the triangle along the bias.

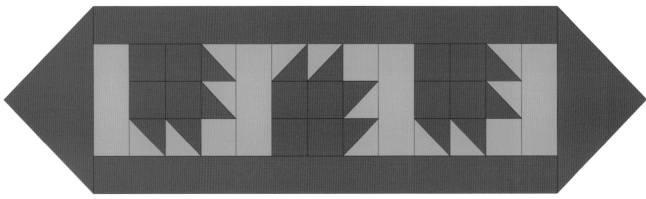

Assembly diagram.

preparing the backing

1 Remove the selvage from the 18" strip of fabric.

2 Join it with the 18" x 20" piece.

- -

finishing your runner

1 Prepare your quilt sandwich following the Layering and Basting instructions on page 15.

2 Quilt.

3 Bind and label your quilt following the instructions on page 16–17.

barrels of fun

Who knew geometry could be so much fun? I love the fact that this simple quilt block has so much going for it. The components of each windmill block are just one rectangle with a sew-and-flip corner. Then, where the blocks come together, another windmill block is formed. But that's not all. The background triangles form a tiny pinwheel! All from that one rectangle with its sew-and-flip corner! If that isn't more fun than a barrel of monkeys, I don't know what is!

choosing fabric

The beauty of this quilt is its versatility. As long as you choose a background that provides contrast with your fat quarters, you'll end up with a successful quilt. If your fat quarters have a lot of design to them, consider choosing a solid, or a fabric that reads as a solid, for the background. The fun monkey fabrics we chose would be perfect for a child's quilt, but don't feel limited to using this pattern only for kids' quilts. Choose something masculine—a wildlife print for the border and coordinating fat quarters for the windmills—for the guy in your life. Set your mind spinning with the possibilities for this one!

The warm browns used in this version give the quilt a country feeling.
Pieced by Monica Solorio-Snow and quilted by the author, 2006.

tip

What are fabrics that "read as solid?" Fabrics that "read as solid" could be tone-on-tone prints that don't have much variation in value or very small prints with small areas of multiple colors. It seems that every fabric company has its own version of a marbled, tone-on-tone or subtle blender print available. When you step back from these fabrics, the pattern shouldn't be obvious, they should look like a solid color. The gentle nuances in these fabrics, however, give life to the block.

The sock monkey fabric seemed perfect for a quilt called Barrels of Fun.
Pieced by Patty Stoltz and quilted by the author, 2006.

measurements

Quilt: 68" x 80"
Block size: 12"

fabric requirements

16 fat quarters
1¾ yd. background
½ yd. dark inner border
1⅓ yd. outer border
⅝ yd. binding
4⅔ yd. backing

cutting instructions

Note: Place the 18" side of the fat quarter along the bottom edge of your cutting mat, selvage at the top.

1. From each fat quarter, cut:
   - (2) 6½" strips; crosscut into (10) 6½" x 3½" rectangles
   - (1) 3½" strip for scrappy middle border
2. From the background fabric, cut:
   - (15) 3½" strips; crosscut into (160) 3½" squares
3. From the inner-border fabric, cut:
   - (6) 2½" strips
4. From the outer-border fabric, cut:
   - (8) 5½" strips
5. From the binding fabric, cut:
   - (8) 2¼" strips

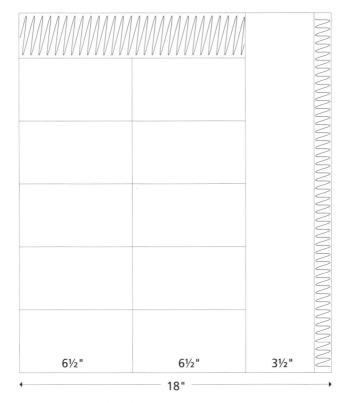

Fat quarter cutting diagram.

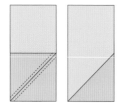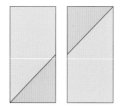

Piecing the windmill blades. *Pairs.*

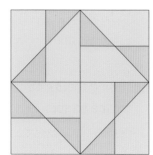

Completed Windmill Block.

Assembly diagram.

piecing the blocks

1 Draw a diagonal line on the wrong side of the 3½" squares.

2 Place a 3½" square, right sides together on one end of a 3½" x 6½" rectangle. Be sure the diagonal line goes from the top left to the bottom right. Stitch on the drawn line.

3 Trim, leaving a ¼" seam allowance. Press toward the darker piece.

4 Repeat to make 160 pieced windmill blades.

Note: You may want to mix up your fabrics at this point. This is a scrappy quilt, and your fabrics should be distributed throughout the top.

5 Join the windmill blades into pairs, keeping the light edges toward the middle.

6 Join four pairs to make a windmill block. Repeat to make 20 blocks.

assembling the top

1 Working on a design wall or on the floor, lay out the blocks in five rows of four blocks. A row of secondary windmill blocks will appear as you lay out the blocks.

2 Once you have the blocks laid out in a pleasing manner, join the blocks together into rows.

3 Press the seams in each row in opposite directions. This will allow the seams in each row to nest with the seams in the row below it.

4 Join the rows together. Press.

adding the borders

1 Join the strips for the contrasting inner border together by sewing diagonal seams. Press open. Join all of the strips together until you have one long strip.

2 Measure the length of your quilt lengthwise through the middle. This will prevent you from having wavy borders. Mathematically, this number would be 60½", but everyone's seam allowances vary, so be sure to measure.

3 Cut two strips the length of your quilt.

4 Attach one to each side of the quilt. Press.

5 Now measure your quilt crosswise through the middle. This measurement should be approximately 52½", but check your measurement to be sure.

6 Cut two strips this length.

7 Add the strips to the top and bottom of your quilt. Press.

8 Repeat steps 1–7 using the 3½" strips cut from the fat quarters for the scrappy middle border.

9 Repeat steps 1–7 with the outer-border fabric for the last border.

preparing the backing

1 Cut the backing fabric into two equal pieces.

2 Remove the selvage and stitch the two pieces together along the longest sides.

finishing your quilt

1 Prepare your quilt sandwich following the Layering and Basting instructions on page 15.

2 A spiral design across the top of this quilt reinforces the idea of spinning windmill blades. It would also be a perfect candidate for stitching in the ditch.

3 Bind and label your quilt following the instructions on page 16–17.

double the fun

The floating diamonds in this quilt may look difficult to construct, but that's only an illusion. Using easy sew-and-flip construction, you end up with perfect squares that go together like a dream. A narrow border of the background fabric makes the diamonds look like they're floating in the middle of the quilt.

When making blocks with sew-and-flip corners, you often trim away quite a bit of fabric. Usually, the ease of construction with this method makes up for the little bit of wasted fabric. With the big blocks in this quilt, however, there is a substantial amount of fabric left on every corner. But, never fear, by adding a second line of stitching, those corners won't be discarded. They'll turn into bonus half-square triangles that can be used in another project! What a perfect way to **Double The Fun**!

choosing fabric

Value and contrast are important for this quilt. The fat quarters you choose should all have the same value. The background fabric should contrast well with the fat quarters so the pattern of the blocks becomes obvious.

A stack of rich brown fat quarters on a light tan background would make a beautiful quilt, as would a group of 1930s reproduction fabrics on a crisp white background. Don't overlook making your background fabric darker than your fat quarters. You might try jewel-toned batiks on a rich black background.

Choose a border that is similar in color and value to the fat quarters you are using. To tie the border of the quilt in nicely with the blocks, you might purchase a little extra and substitute it for one of the fat quarters. Binding that matches the border is a good choice for this quilt.

Lively polka dots dance across the surface of this version of the quilt.
Pieced and quilted by the author, 2006.

The combination of large and small diamonds adds visual interest to this quilt.
Pieced by Monica Solorio-Snow and quilted by the author, 2006.

measurements

Quilt: 68" x 88"
Block size: 10"

fabric requirements

15 fat quarters
Note: You'll need fat quarters that are at least 17½" x 19½" for this project. If you don't have quite that much usable fabric in each fat quarter, add a few more to the mix.

4 yd. background fabric
⅓ yd. contrasting inner border
1¾ yd. outer border
⅔ yd. binding
5¼ yd. backing

cutting instructions

Note: Place the 18" side of the fat quarter along the bottom edge of your cutting mat, selvage at the top.

1. From each fat quarter, cut:
   (1) 4½" strip; crosscut into (4) 4½" squares
   (2) 6½" strips; crosscut into (5) 6½" squares and
       (1) 4½" square

2. From the background fabric, cut:
   (8) 10½" strips; crosscut each strip into
       (3) 10½" squares and
       (1) 10½" x 6½" rectangle
   (2) 10½" strips; crosscut each strip into
       (6) 10½" x 6½" rectangles
   (1) 6½" strip; crosscut into (4) 6½" squares
   (7) 2½" strips for border
3. From the contrasting inner-border fabric, cut:
   (9) 1½" strips
4. From the outer-border fabric, cut:
   (9) 6½" strips
5. From the binding fabric, cut:
   (9) 2¼" strips

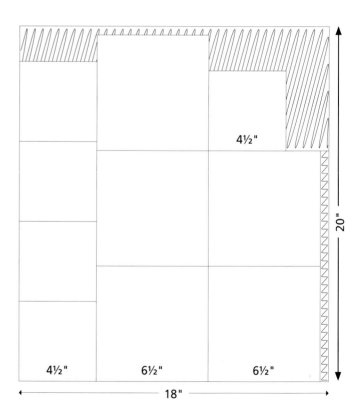

Fat quarter cutting diagram.

piecing the blocks

Note: This quilt is made up from four different blocks, the full block, the half block, the half block reversed and the quarter block.

Full Block

1 Draw a diagonal line on the wrong sides of the 6½" and 4½" squares.

2 Place a 4½" square on one corner of a 10½" square, right sides together. Sew on the marked line. Before cutting, sew a second line of stitching ½" from the drawn line.

3 Cut apart between the two stitched lines. Set the small, pieced square aside. You will use it later in the bonus quilt.

4 Choosing fabrics at random, repeat steps 2 and 3, adding a 4½" square to the opposite corner. Press open.

5 Add 6½" squares to the remaining two corners, stitching on the line and ½" away before cutting and pressing.

6 Repeat steps 1–5 to make 24 blocks.

Stitch two lines, ½" apart before cutting.

4½" squares sewn to opposite corners.

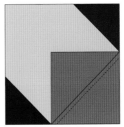

Adding the 6½" corners.

Completed full block.

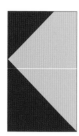

Half block.

Half block reversed.

Corner block.

Half Block

7 Place a 4½" square on the upper left corner of a 6½" x 10½" background rectangle. Sew with two lines of stitching. Cut and press.

8 Place a 6½" square on the lower left corner. Sew with two lines of stitching. Cut and press.

9 Repeat Steps 7 and 8 to make 10 half blocks.

Half Block Reversed

10 Place a 6½" square on the upper left corner of a 6½" x 10½" background rectangle. Sew with two lines of stitching. Cut and press.

11 Place a 4½" square on the upper right corner of a 6½" x 10½" background rectangle. Sew with two lines of stitching. Cut and press.

12 Repeat steps 11 and 12 to make 10 half blocks reversed.

Corner Block

13 Place a 6½" background square together with a 6½" print square. Sew with a double line.

14 Cut and press.

15 Repeat Steps 13 and 14 to make 4 corner blocks.

assembling the top

1 Working on a design wall or on the floor, lay out the full blocks, half blocks and corner blocks as shown in the assembly diagram.

2 Once you have the blocks laid out in a pleasing manner, join the blocks together into rows.

3 Press the seams in each row in opposite directions. This will allow the seams in each row to nest with the seams in the row below it.

4 Join the rows together. Press.

Assembly diagram.

adding the borders

1 Join the strips for the inner border together by sewing diagonal seams. Press open. Join all of the strips together until you have one long strip.

2 Measure the length of your quilt lengthwise through the middle. This will prevent you from having wavy borders. Mathematically, this number would be 70½", but everyone's seam allowances vary, so be sure to measure.

3 Cut two strips the length of your quilt.

4 Attach one to each side of the quilt. Press.

5 Now measure your quilt crosswise through the middle. This measurement should be approximately 54½", but check your measurement to be sure.

6 Cut two strips this length.

7 Add the strips to the top and bottom of your quilt. Press.

8 Repeat steps 1–7 with your contrasting inner-border fabric.

9 Repeat steps 1–7 with your outer-border fabric.

preparing the backing

1 Cut the backing fabric into two equal pieces.

2 Remove the selvage and stitch the two pieces together along the longest sides.

finishing your quilt

1 Prepare your quilt sandwich following the Layering and Basting instructions on page 15.

2 You may want to quilt your background fabrics with a different colored thread than the blocks in your quilt. Or, you could choose a variegated thread for use with an allover design. The background squares are large enough for some special quilting.

3 Bind and label your quilt following the instructions on page 16–17.

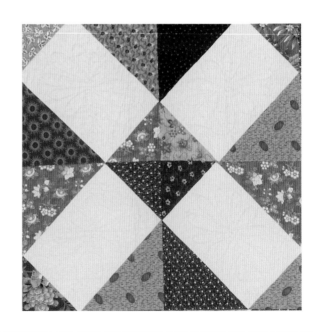

bonus quilt

The half-square triangles left from creating the large quilt can be pieced into a charming second quilt.

Pieced by Monica Solorio-Snow and quilted by the author, 2006.

It's easy to use all the pieces trimmed from your quilt for a second project. It makes a nice sized quilt, and doesn't require much effort at all!

measurements

Quilt: 40" x 48"
Block size: 4"

fabric requirements

Half-square triangles left over from Double the Fun.
 1 yd. additional background fabric for borders
 (4) 2½" squares cut from fat quarter scraps
 ½ yd. binding
 1½ yd. backing

cutting instructions

1. From the background fabric, cut:
 (9) 2½" strips for the inner and outer borders
2. From the binding fabric, cut:
 (6) 2¼" strips

piecing the blocks

Large quarter-square triangles

1 Draw a diagonal line on half of the large half square triangles.

2 Place two large half-square triangles right sides together—one marked and one unmarked. The background fabric on the top block should be facing the print fabric on the bottom block. Nest seams together.

3 Stitch ¼" on either side of the marked line. Cut on the drawn line, yielding two quarter-square triangles.

Quarter-square triangles.

4 Press and square up to 4½".

5 Repeat to make 63 quarter-square triangles.

Small Quarter-square Triangles for Border

1 Repeat steps 1–3 above to make quarter-square triangles from the small leftover blocks.

2 Square up to 2½".

3 Make 72 quarter-square triangles.

assembling the top

1 Working on a design wall or on the floor, lay out the large quarter-square triangles, alternating the direction of each block, as shown in the assembly diagram.

2 Once you have the blocks laid out in a pleasing manner, join the blocks together into rows.

3 Press the seams in each row in opposite directions. This will allow the seams in each row to nest with the seams in the row below it.

4 Join the rows together. Press.

Assembly diagram.

making the pieced border

Note: The border blocks are set together so that the background fabric forms a diamond. By adding a strip of background fabric to each side of the pieced border, it will appear to "float" around the outside edge of the quilt.

1 Join 20 quarter-square blocks together into a strip for the side of the quilt.

2 Repeat to make a second strip.

3 Join 16 quarter-square triangles together into a strip for the top of the quilt.

4 Repeat to make a second strip for the bottom.

5 To each end of the top and bottom strips, add a 2½" square cut from fat quarter scraps.

adding the inner border

1 Join the background border strips together by sewing diagonal seams. Press open. Join all of the strips together until you have one long strip.

2 Add a 63½" background border strip to each side of the quilt. Press.

3 Add a 32½" background border strip to the top and bottom of the quilt. Press.

adding the pieced border

1 Add a long pieced border strip to each side of the quilt. Press.

2 Add a short pieced border strip to the top and bottom of the quilt. Press.

adding the outer border

1 Use the remaining pieced strip left from the inner-background border.

2 Measure the length of your quilt lengthwise through the middle. This will prevent you from having wavy borders.

3 Cut two strips the length of your quilt.

4 Attach one to each side of the quilt. Press.

5 Now measure your quilt crosswise through the middle.

6 Cut two strips this length.

7 Add the strips to the top and bottom of your quilt. Press.

preparing the backing

1 One length of fabric should be wide enough for the back of this quilt.

finishing your quilt

1 Prepare your quilt sandwich following the Layering and Basting instructions on page 15.

2 Diagonal quilting in the ditch would be an easy finish for this quilt. You could also stipple the entire quilt or stipple only in the background to make the other fabrics stand out more.

3 Bind and label your quilt following the instructions on page 16–17.

The stunning results you'll achieve with this pattern belie the ease of construction. The placement of lights and darks is alternated in each block. When all the blocks are stitched together, an amazing thing will happen—you'll be seeing stars. Now that's *Funtastic*!

choosing fabric

Contrast is an important feature in this quilt. The fat quarters you choose should all be of a medium dark to dark value. Then choose a background fabric that will provide a good contrast. If your fat quarters tend to be more in the medium range, perhaps a very dark background would be appropriate.

Soft, muted florals on a dark green background would make a lovely quilt with this pattern. Hot colors—reds, oranges, bright yellows and pinks—on a strong green background would be equally successful and create an entirely different look.

The pieced border will "float" around the outside edge of your quilt because it is flanked by additional borders of the background fabric. When choosing the narrow inner border, pick something that will separate the blocks from the borders. The fat quarters will provide enough fabric for a scrappy binding, or you could purchase an additional ⅝ yd. of the inner-border fabric for a solid binding.

A multitude of colors dance across the top of this quilt.
Pieced by Carol Osterholm and quilted by the author, 2006.

The mottled tones in this background print make it appear as though more than one fabric was used.
Pieced and quilted by the author, 2006.

measurements

Quilt: 81" x 91"
Block size: 5"

fabric requirements

18 fat quarters
4½ yd. background
⅔ yd. contrasting inner border
binding (left over from fat quarters)
5½ yd. backing fabric

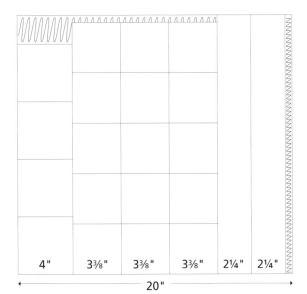

| 4" | 3⅜" | 3⅜" | 3⅜" | 2¼" | 2¼" |

← 20" →

Fat quarter cutting diagram.

cutting instructions

Note: Place the 20" side of the fat quarter along the bottom edge of your cutting mat, selvage at the right.

1. From each fat quarter, cut:
   (1) 4" strip; crosscut into (4) 4" squares
   (3) 3⅜" strips; crosscut each into (15) 3⅜" square
   Cut each square in half diagonally
   (2) 2¼" strips for binding
2. From the background fabric, cut:
   (14) 4" strips; crosscut each strip into (10) 4" squares
   (13) 3⅜" strips; crosscut each strip into (11) 3⅜" squares
   Cut each square in half diagonally
   (16) 3½" strips for inner and outer borders
3. From the contrasting inner-border fabric, cut:
   (7) 2½" strips

piecing the blocks

Light squares

1 Stitch dark triangles to opposite sides of a 4" background square. Press.

2 Stitch dark triangles to the remaining two sides. Press. Make 132.

Light squares.

Dark Squares

1 Stitch background triangles to opposite sides of a dark 4" square. Press.

2 Stitch background triangles to the remaining two sides. Press. Make 71.

Dark squares.

tip

For easier construction when making a square-in-a-square block, always sew the first two triangles to opposite sides of the center squares, rather than in a clockwise fashion. You'll find it easier to match the center points this way.

assembling the top

1 Working on a design wall or on the floor, lay out the blocks in 13 rows of 11 blocks, starting every other row with a light block as shown in the assembly diagram. You will have 60 light blocks left over for the pieced border.

2 Once you have the blocks laid out in a pleasing manner, join the blocks together into rows.

3 Press the seams in each row in opposite directions. This will allow the seams in each row to nest with the seams in the row below it.

4 Join the rows together. Press.

Assembly diagram.

making the pieced border

1 Join light blocks together in four strips. Each strip will have 15 blocks.

adding the borders

1 Join the strips for the contrasting inner border together by sewing diagonal seams. Press open. Join all of the strips together until you have one long strip.

2 Measure the length of your quilt lengthwise through the middle. This will prevent you from having wavy borders. Mathematically, this number would be 65½", but everyone's seam allowances vary, so be sure to measure.

3 Cut two strips the length of your quilt.

4 Attach a strip to each side of the quilt. Press.

5 Now measure your quilt crosswise through the middle. This measurement should be approximately 65½", but check your measurement to be sure.

6 Cut two strips this length.

7 Add the strips to the top and bottom of your quilt. Press.

8 Repeat steps 1–7 with seven strips of the background fabric for the next border.

9 Add the pieced border, first to the sides, then the top and bottom. If necessary, make adjustments in length before adding these borders.

10 Repeat steps 1–7 with nine strips of the background fabric for the last border.

preparing the backing

1 Cut the backing fabric into two equal pieces.

2 Remove the selvage and stitch the two pieces together along the longest sides.

finishing your quilt

1 Prepare your quilt sandwich following the Layering and Basting instructions on page 15.

2 To give dimension to your quilt, you may choose to stipple in the dark or light squares rather than both. You could also follow the diagonal design and quilt in the ditch. The koi in the smaller version inspired me to quilt a design that looked like water across the quilt.

3 Bind and label your quilt following the instructions on page 16–17.

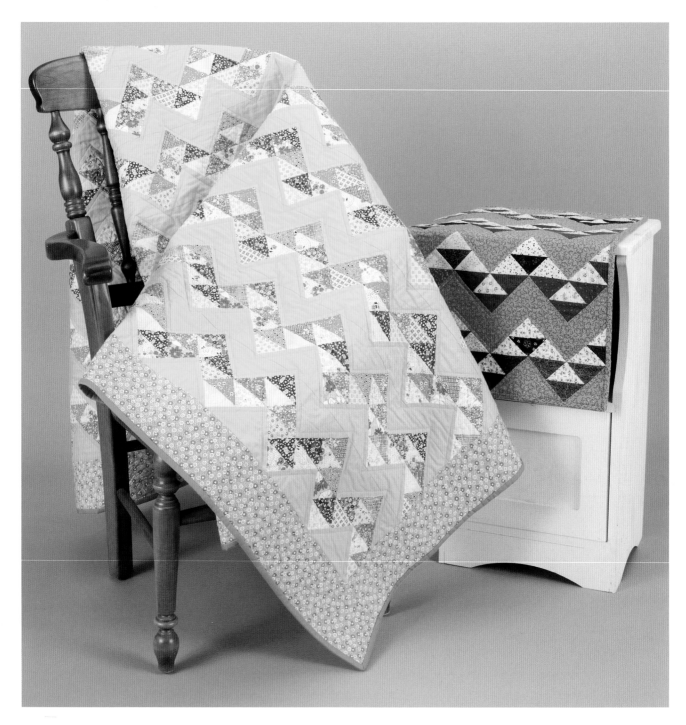

The inspiration for this quilt was a photograph of an antique quilt—its strong, geometric design really appealed to me. I'm always amazed at the wonderful quilts that were created before rotary cutting and quick piecing techniques. Make this quilt today and you'll have *Sew Much Fun*!

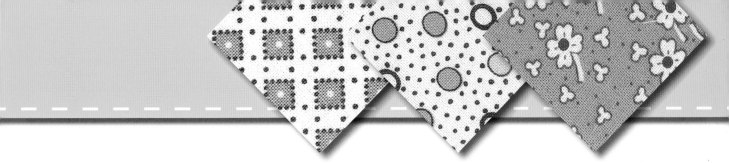

choosing fabric

Value is more important than color when choosing the fat quarters for this quilt. You will need both light and dark fat quarters. You must also consider the accent fabric. It should be able to stand out from both the light and dark fabrics in the fat quarters. This can be accomplished by choosing a fabric in a medium value, or a color that doesn't appear in the other fabrics. A solid or monochromatic print works best for the accent fabric.

While this quilt is perfect for the 1930s reproduction prints used here, it would also be stunning in bold, bright colors with a lime green or turquoise accent fabric. A turn-of-the-century or Civil War palette, as shown in the small version, would also be appropriate.

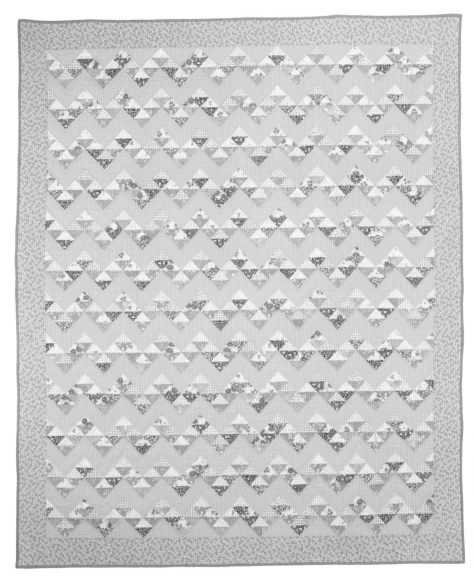

In this version, which uses reproduction prints from the late nineteenth century, the contrast in the blue prints and light shirtings is more obvious. The lights and darks used in the pieced triangles are the same within each unit, and the borders are omitted.
Pieced and quilted by the author, 2006.

The lights and darks used in the pieced triangles aren't as apparent in this version of the quilt, as is often the case with 1930s prints. However, the "screaming yellow" solid keeps the palette from being too soft.
Pieced by Beverly Wakeman and quilted by the author, 2006.

measurements

Quilt: 64½" x 75¾"

fabric requirements

9 light fat quarters
9 dark fat quarters
2⅓ yd. accent fabric
1⅛ yd. outer
⅝ yd. binding
4 yd. backing

cutting instructions

Note: Place the 20" side of the fat quarter along the bottom edge of your cutting mat, selvage at the right.

1. From each fat quarter, cut:
   (6) 2⅞" strips; crosscut each strip into (5) 2⅞" squares
2. Set aside 252 squares (14 per fat quarter). Set aside an equal amount of dark and light squares.
3. Cut the remaining squares in half once diagonally.
4. From the accent fabric, cut:
   (11) 7" strips; crosscut each strip into (6) 7" squares.
   Cut each square in half twice diagonally.
5. From the border fabric, cut:
   (8) 4½" strips
6. From the binding fabric, cut:
   (8) 2¼" strips

Cutting accent triangles.

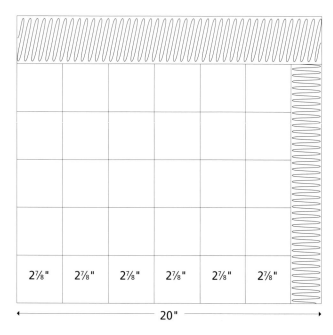

| 2⅞" | 2⅞" | 2⅞" | 2⅞" | 2⅞" | 2⅞" |

← 20" →

Fat quarter cutting diagram.

piecing the blocks

1 Draw a diagonal line on the wrong side of the light 2⅞" squares.

2 Randomly pair a light square with a dark square, right sides together, and sew ¼" on either side of the marked line.

3 Cut apart on the marked line. Press toward the dark fabric.

Pieced squares.

4 Repeat with all the squares, making 252 pieced squares.

tip

Mixing the light and dark triangles before piecing and choosing them randomly as you piece the triangle units will result in a scrappy look. For a more organized, calmer effect, each pieced triangle unit could be made using the same three light or dark fabrics.

Light Pieced Triangles

5 To one dark side of a pieced square, add a light triangle. Press away from the square.

6 Add another light triangle to the remaining dark side of the pieced square. Press away from the square.

7 Repeat Steps 5 and 6 to make 132 light triangles.

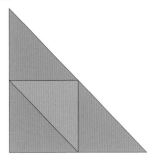

Light pieced triangles.

Dark Pieced Triangles

8 To one light side of a pieced square, add a dark triangle. Press away from the square.

9 Add another dark triangle to the remaining light side of the pieced square. Press away from the square.

10 Repeat Steps 8 and 9 to make 120 light triangles.

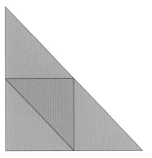

Dark pieced triangles.

piecing the rows

Note: Each row is actually a double row, with light pieced triangles in the top half and dark pieced triangles in the bottom half.

1 For the top half of the row, join 10 accent triangles with 11 light pieced triangles, starting and ending with a pieced triangle. Press toward the accent triangle.

2 For the bottom half of the row, join 11 accent triangles with 10 dark pieced triangles, starting and ending with an accent triangle. Press toward the accent triangle.

3 Join the top and bottom halves together. Press.

Note: The ends of the rows will be uneven at this point.

4 Repeat to make 12 rows.

tips

When joining the accent triangles together with the pieced triangles, the ends need to be offset by a quarter inch. There are tools on the market which can help you trim the quarter inch from the points before sewing, making lining up the patches a breeze.

You will be working with bias edges and straight-of-grain edges. Bias edges are formed when fabric has been cut on the diagonal. The bias edge has more give and will stretch more than the straight-of-grain edge. You must take care not to stretch the bias edge when handling and pressing the patches. When possible, if you are joining a patch with a bias edge to a patch with a straight-of-grain edge, put the bias edged patch on the bottom when feeding through your sewing machine.

assembling the top

1 Join the 12 rows together, being sure to keep the light pieced triangles on the top in each row. The edges of the quilt top will be uneven.

2 Stay stitch in a straight line along both sides of the quilt. This line of stitching should be approximately ⅛" outside the triangle points.

3 Trim edges even, leaving a ¼" seam allowance.

4 Stay stitch the edges of the quilt top.

tip

Stay stitching stabilizes the edges of your quilt top. When you trim the uneven edges of the quilt, you will be leaving bias edges that will have a tendency to stretch. When you stay stitch a scant ¼" from the edge, your quilt top won't stretch when you add the borders. This line of stitching will be covered when you apply your binding.

Assembly diagram.

adding the borders

1 Join the strips for the border together by sewing diagonal seams. Press open. Join all of the strips together until you have one long strip.

2 Measure the length of your quilt lengthwise through the middle. This will prevent you from having wavy borders. Mathematically, this number would be 67½", but everyone's seam allowances vary, so be sure to measure.

3 Cut two strips the length of your quilt.

4 Attach a strip to each side of the quilt. Press.

5 Now measure your quilt crosswise through the middle. This measurement should be approximately 64½", but check your measurement to be sure.

6 Cut two strips this length.

7 Add the strips to the top and bottom of your quilt. Press.

preparing the backing

1 Cut the backing fabric into two equal pieces.

2 Remove the selvage and stitch the two pieces together along the longest sides. The seam will run crosswise on the back of the quilt.

finishing your quilt

1 Prepare your quilt sandwich following the Layering and Basting instructions on page 15.

2 Whether quilting by hand or machine, quilting one quarter inch from the seam lines on the accent fabric is a perfect choice for this quilt and reinforces the strong, geometric lines of the quilt. The pieced triangles could be stitched in the ditch or stippled.

3 Bind and label your quilt following the instructions on page 16–17.

Fat Quarter Fun is Karen Snyder's second book. It follows the popular *Bundles of Fun*. Besides designing quilts and authoring books, Karen owns Anna Lena's Quilt Shop and designs 1930s reproduction fabrics—called Wash Tub Prints—for Andover Fabrics.

Although she always knew that she would someday be a quilter, Karen didn't start quilting until 1995 when she received a free quilt pattern in the mail. Once she started hand piecing that Grandmother's Flower Garden, she was hooked and hasn't looked back.

Karen lives in Long Beach, Washington, with her husband, Bob Hamilton.

Anna Lena's Quilt Shop
PO Box 1399
111 Bolstad Avenue
Long Beach, WA 98631
(360) 642-8585
www.annalena.com

Annie's Attic
1 Annie Lane
Big Sandy, TX 75755
(800) 582-6643
www.anniesattic.com

Keepsake Quilting
Route 25
P.O. Box 1618
Center Harbor, NH 03226-1618
(800) 438-5464
www.keepsakequilting.com

Krause Publications
(888) 457-2873
www.krause.com

More Fantastic Uses for Fat Quarters

Quilt As Desired
*Your Guide to Straight-Line and
Free-Motion Quilting*
by Charlene C. Frable

Avoid the frustration of nearing the end of a project, only to see the dreaded phrase "quilt as desired" staring at you. Turn to this revolutionary guide for the answers to that one phrase, while you create six projects using straight-line and free-motion techniques.

Hardcover • 8¼ x 10⅞ • 128 pages
150 color photos
Item# Z0743 • $24.99

Bundles of Fun
Quilts From Fat Quarters
by Karen Snyder

Discover fabric selection advice, instructions for making quilts and for adding sashing and borders. Offers variations for 12 coordinating projects.

Softcover • 8¼ x 10⅞ • 128 pages
150+ color photos and illus.
Item# FQLQ • $22.99

Fat Quarter Small Quilts
25 Projects You Can Make in a Day
by Darlene Zimmerman

Use the stack of fat quarter scraps in your sewing room to complete 25 spectacular projects including wall hangings, tablemats, doll quilts, gifts and more in a wide variety of themes. Most projects can be completed in less than a day!

Softcover • 8¼ x 10⅞ • 128 pages
250 color photos and illus.
Item# FQSM • $21.99

**Call 800-258-0929
to order today!
Offer CRB7**

Krause Publications, Offer CRB7
PO Box 5009, Iola, WI 54945-5009
www.krausebooks.com

Order directly from the publisher by calling 800-258-0929 M-F 8 am – 5 pm

Online at www.krausebooks.com or from booksellers and craft and fabric shops nationwide.

Please reference offer CRB7 with all direct-to-publisher orders.

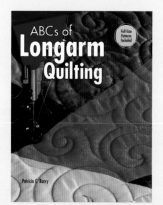

ABCs of Longarm Quilting
by Patricia C. Barry

Learn all about longarm quilting from one of the country's best quilters, and you'll be on your way to personal success, and possibly a business venture. From detailed instructions for basic techniques, full-size patterns, and expert business advice, to the 150 color photos and four projects in this book, you'll walk away with the know-how to make the most of your longarm quilting.

Hardcover • 8¼ x 10⅞ • 128 pages
200+ color photos
Item# Z0614 • $27.99

90-Minute Quilts
*25+ Projects You Can Make
in an Afternoon*
by Meryl Ann Butler

Discover how easy it is to create stylish baby quilts and large lap quilts, plus wall hangings using the quick tips, methods and 250 how-to color photos and illustrations included in this read-as-you-work book.

Hardcover • 8 x 8 • 160 pages
250 color photos and illus.
Item# NTYMQ • $24.99